Tantra in Tibet

D1252197

THE WISDOM OF TIBET SERIES

The Buddhism of Tibet
H.H. the Dalai Lama

Tantra in Tibet
H.H. the Dalai Lama
Tsong-ka-pa
Jeffrey Hopkins

Deity Yoga
H.H. the Dalai Lama
Tsong-ka-pa
Jeffrey Hopkins

Tantra in Tibet

H.H. the Dalai Lama, Tsong-ka-pa
and Jeffrey Hopkins

•

Translated and Edited by Jeffrey Hopkins

Associate editor for the Dalai Lama's text and
Tsong-ka-pa's text: Lati Rinbochay

Associate editor Tsong-ka-pa's text: Geshe Gedun Lodro

Assistant editor for the Dalai Lama's text: Barbara Frye

Snow Lion Publications
Ithaca, New York USA

Snow Lion Publications
P.O. Box 6483
Ithaca, New York 14851
USA

Printed in USA

ISBN 0-937938-49-1

Library of Congress Cataloging-in-Publication Data

Tson-kha-pa Blo-bzan-grags-pa, 1357–1419
    Tantra in Tibet.

    Reprint. Originally published: London ;
Boston : Allen & Unwin, 1977.
    Translation of selections from: Snags rim chen po.
    Bibliography: p.
    Includes index.
    1. Dge-lugs-pa (Sect)—Doctrines—Early works
to 1800. 2. Tantric Buddhism—China—Tibet—
Doctrines—Early works to 1800. I. Bstan-'dzin-rgya-
mtsho, Dalai Lama XIV, 1935–   . II. Hopkins,
Jeffrey. III. Title.
BQ7950.T754S572513   1987 b   294.3'925   87–16561
ISBN 0–937938–49–1

*Published under the aegis of
the Library of Tibetan Works and Archives
with the authority of
His Holiness the Dalai Lama
as revealing oral tradition*

*May whatever merit there is in presenting
this book on tantra serve to benefit each
and every sentient being throughout space.*

Editor's Note

Homage to Vajradhara.

The Great Exposition of Secret Mantra by Tsong-ka-pa (1357–1419), founder of the Gelukpa order of Tibetan Buddhism, presents the main features of all the Buddhist tantra systems as well as the difference between sutra and tantra, the two divisions of Buddha's word. In 1972 when I was in Dharamsala, northern India, on a Fulbright Fellowship, His Holiness the Dalai Lama asked me to translate *The Great Exposition of Secret Mantra,* the first section of which is the second part of this book. The first part is the Dalai Lama's own commentary which he graciously consented to give in August 1974, upon my return to Dharamsala. His commentary, which was recorded, translated and edited, provides invaluable insight into tantra in general and Tsong-ka-pa's work in particular. Presenting the rich Tibetan oral tradition, his words reveal the highly practical and compassionate use of this ancient science of spiritual development.

The third part of the book is a short supplement which I hope will clarify three key points of Tsong-ka-pa's teaching. The supplement is drawn from the oral teachings of Kensur Lekden (1900–71), abbot of the Tantric College of Lower Lhasa, and Professor Geshe Gedün Lodrö of the University of Hamburg as well as from general explanations of tantra found in each of the four orders of Tibetan Buddhism:

Nyingma
> Long-chen-rap-jam's *Precious Treasury of the Supreme Vehicle* and *Treasury of Tenets*;

Kagyu
> Pad-ma-kar-po's *General Presentation of the Tantra Sets, Captivating the Wise*;

Sakya

   Sö-nam-tse-mo's *General Presentation of the Tantra Sets;*

   Bu-tön's *General Presentation of the Tantra Sets— condensed, middling and extensive versions;*

Geluk

   Lo-sang-chö-ki-gye-tsen's *Presentation of the General Teaching and the Four Tantra Sets;*

   Long-dol Ngak-wang-lo-sang's *Terminology Arising in Secret Mantra, the Scriptural Division of the Knowledge Bearers;*

   Pa-bong-ka-pa's *Miscellaneous Notes from Jo-nay Pandita's Explanation of the Great Exposition of Secret Mantra.*

The first two parts were orally re-translated into Tibetan for Lati Rinpochay, a philosophy master and tantric lama from the Dalai Lama's monastery in Dharamsala, for the sake of correction and verification. Geshe Gedün Lodrö, a Tibetan scholar of scholars at present teaching at the University of Hamburg, provided invaluable information and interpretation for the translation of Tsong-ka-pa's text. Barbara Frye, a student of Tibetan Buddhism for several years, provided crucial help in editing the Dalai Lama's commentary.

A guide to Tsong-ka-pa's text, following his own mode of division of the contents, is given in tabular form in an appendix. The eight chapter divisions and their titles in the Dalai Lama's commentary and in Tsong-ka-pa's text were added to facilitate understanding. The transliteration scheme for Sanskrit names and titles is aimed at easy pronunciation, using *sh*, *ṣh*, and *ch* rather than *ś*, *ṣ*, and *c*. With the first occurrence of each Indian title, the Sanskrit is given, if available. Often Tsong-ka-pa refers only to the title or the author of a work, whereas both are given in translation to obviate the need for checking back and forth.

9

The full Sanskrit and Tibetan titles are to be found in the bibliography, which is arranged alphabetically according to the English titles of sutras and tantras and according to the authors of other works. The Sanskrit and Tibetan originals of key terms have been given in a glossary at the end.

Charlottesville, Virginia   JEFFREY HOPKINS

Acknowledgement

We wish to thank Mr Gerald Yorke for many suggestions which improved the rendering in English of Part II.

Contents

11

I
Essence of Tantra

by
His Holiness
TENZIN GYATSO
The Fourteenth Dalai Lama

Translated and edited by Jeffrey Hopkins
Associate editor: Lati Rinpochay
Assistant editor: Barbara Frye

Tantra For Practice

It is essential to settle the meaning of the scriptures with stainless reasoning. The meaning of passages that are spoken only for certain trainees must be interpreted and the meaning of extremely subtle passages must be penetrated; this is difficult, and some are in danger of misunderstanding. Also, for many the countless books of sutra and tantra do not appear as precepts, and they are satisfied with seeing only a fraction of the path. Others are able to analyse a great many points but are unable, even though they are learned, to discern the important ones. They know, in general, how to practise but do not make any effort at practice. Those in these three situations cannot practise tantra properly.

Tsong-ka-pa saw that if the meanings of the countless scriptures were collected, settled with stainless reasoning, and set forth in the sequence of their practice, many sentient beings who had come under the influence of these bad circumstances would be helped. Captivated by the good explanations of the Indian and Tibetan tantrics such as Nagarjuna, his spiritual sons and the omniscient Bu-tön (Bu-ston), Tsong-ka-pa was enthused to gather together these explanations in order to rectify the faults and omissions existing in the presentations by earlier lamas.

Writing a book on Secret Mantra is not like writing a book on Madhyamika or on the teachings of the paths contained in the *Perfection of Wisdom Sutras (Prajñāpāramitā)*. The topics of Secret Mantra are not to be displayed like merchandise but practised secretly. If they are not, instead of helping, there is a danger of harming many people due to generating misunderstanding. For instance, some who are unable to practise the four tantras

15

in general and Highest Yoga Tantra in particular merely wish to play with Mantra. Some, although they have faith, do not accurately know the Buddhist presentations of view, meditation, and behaviour. Others know these topics accurately but do not have an ability to maintain vows, sustain faith, and be strong of mind. Without this knowledge and this ability, practice of the Mantra path is impossible.

In India a fully qualified guru taught the doctrines of Secret Mantra to only a few students, whose karma and aspirations were suitable and whom he knew well. The gurus passed the doctrines directly to their students, and when the students were able to practise with great effort the teachings that they received, the corresponding spiritual experiences and realisations were generated. In just that measure the Conqueror's teaching was furthered and the welfare of sentient beings was achieved. However, in the snowy country of Tibet these factors were largely absent. Secret Mantra was disseminated too widely and people sought it because of its fame, without considering whether they had the capacity to practise it or not.

One is wise if, though wanting the best, one examines whether the best is fitting. The Tibetans wanted the best and assumed that they could practise the best. As a result of this, Secret Mantra became famous in Tibet, but the mode of practice was not like the proper hidden practice of the Indians and thus we were unable to achieve the feats of Secret Mantra as explained in the tantras; the imprint of Secret Mantra practice did not appear. As it is said in the Tibetan oral tradition, 'An Indian practises one deity and achieves a hundred; a Tibetan practises a hundred deities and does not achieve even one.'

It is not good to begin many different works, saying 'This looks good; that looks good', touching this, touching that, and not succeeding in any of them. If you do not generate great desires but aim at what is fitting, you can actualise the corresponding potencies and become an expert in that. With success, the power or imprint of that practice is generated.

Especially nowadays, Secret Mantra has become a topic of interest, but merely as an object of inquiry. From the viewpoint of a practitioner, it seems to have become an object of entertainment and to have arrived at the point where one cannot know whether it will help or harm. Many of the secrets have been disseminated; many lecturers are explaining tantra, and books are being translated. Even though Secret Mantra is to be achieved in hiding, many books have appeared that are a mixture of truth and falsity.

I think it would be good if the means and circumstances appeared which could clear away these wrong ideas. In general, translating a book of Mantra for sale in the shops is unsuitable, but at this time and in this situation there is greater fault in not clearing away wrong ideas than there is in distributing translations. Much falsely ascribed information about Secret Mantra has wide repute nowadays, and, therefore, I think that translating and distributing an authoritative book may help to clear away these false superimpositions. This is the reason for my explanation of Tsong-ka-pa's work.

If Secret Mantra is practised openly and used for commercial purposes, then accidents will befall such a practitioner, even taking his life, and conditions unfavourable for generating spiritual experience and realisations in his continuum will be generated. With other books it is not too serious to make an error, but with books of Mantra it is very serious to err either in explanation or in translation. Furthermore, if the fault of proclaiming the secret to those who are not ripened is incurred, there is danger that instead of helping, it will harm. There are many stories of people who have begun treatises on Mantra but have been unable to complete their lifespan and

17

of others whose progress was delayed through writing a book on Mantra.

A person who has practised the stages of sutra and wishes to attain quickly the state of a blessed Buddha *should* enter into the Secret Mantra Vehicle that can easily bestow realisation of Buddhahood. However, you cannot seek Buddhahood for yourself, engaging in Mantra in order to become unusual. With a spiritual guide as a protector, you need to train in the common paths, engaging in the practices of beings of small and middling capacity—recognising suffering and developing a wish to leave cyclic existence. Then you must train in the compassion that is the inability to bear the sight of suffering in others without acting to relieve it. Beings want happiness but are bereft of happiness; they do not want suffering but are tortured by suffering. You must develop great compassion and mercy from the very orb of your heart for all sentient beings travelling in cyclic existence in the three realms—desire, form, and formless. You need to have a very strong mind wishing to free all sentient beings from suffering and its causes.

Through the force of having accumulated predispositions over many lifetimes, some persons have a good mind even when young; they have unbearable compassion for insects who are in danger of dying and for humans stricken with suffering; they have a keen sense of altruism. Such persons should enter the Mantra Vehicle in order to attain Buddhahood quickly.

Not all persons can practise tantra, but someone who has performed good actions over many lifetimes, who even as a child possessed a strong thought to help, and who has good predispositions should seek the aid of a spiritual guide. Through his quintessential instructions, the student should, with effort and over a period of months and years, raise this good mind to higher and higher levels. Finally, whether going, wandering, lying, or sitting, he has a strong force of mind seeking to do whatever can be done to help others. He wishes very strongly to bring vast help to others in a spontaneous manner, effortlessly, as a Buddha. Such a person is suitable to enter and *should* enter Secret Mantra in order to attain Buddhahood quickly.

If you are seeking a mere temporary sufficiency of food and clothing for yourself and others, seeking only the temporary purposes of this lifetime, avoiding temporary disease, attaining affluence of resources or a temporary good name or a great deal of money, certainly there are means for the temporary achievement of great wealth, for temporarily relieving sickness and disease, and for achieving temporary fame. You can be greedy and deceptive, sometimes being honest and at other times lying, sometimes fighting and at other times not. These are temporary means, and nowadays many people are proceeding in this way. If this is your intention, you have no need for Tsong-ka-pa's *Great Exposition of Secret Mantra*.

If, on the other hand, you do not take this system of the elders of the world to be sufficient, if you view such activities as senseless, pithless, if you know that they do not help future lives or higher aims, if you know that even in terms of this life no matter how wealthy you become, it is difficult to have peace of mind, and if you are seeking peace of mind for yourself and others, it is very important to improve your mind.

Many have given precepts for this purpose, but we say that only the teacher Buddha taught forcefully that we should cherish others more than ourselves and that we should develop an intention definitely to establish sentient beings in a state free from suffering and the causes of suffering. All of the world's religious systems teach a means of bringing a little peace to the mind and cleansing coarser aspects of the mental continuum. They either

19

directly or indirectly create improvement in terms of a good mind and of altruism, but among them it seems that only Buddhism presents, by way of a vast number of reasonings, scriptures, and views, the means of transforming the mind into ultimate goodness. I am not saying that Buddhism is best because I am a Buddhist. I think that if it is considered honestly one would think so, but, even if it is the best, this does not mean that everyone should be a Buddhist. All do not have the same disposition and interest. All should have the best, but since not all are capable of practising the best it is necessary for each person to observe a path that accords with his own disposition, interest, and ability.

If it were true that everyone should be a Buddhist, that everyone should be a Tantrist, and that everyone should follow Highest Yoga Tantra because it is the best, then Vajradhara would have taught only Highest Yoga Tantra. He would indeed have done so if everyone were capable of practising it. But for those for whom Highest Yoga Tantra was not suitable he taught Yoga Tantra. For those for whom Yoga Tantra was not suitable he taught Performance Tantra. For those for whom Performance Tantra was not suitable he taught Action Tantra. Those for whom Action Tantra was not suitable he taught by way of sutra in which not even the name of 'Secret Mantra' occurs.

Within sutra he taught the *Perfection of Wisdom Sutras* setting forth the Madhyamika view, and for those for whom this was not suitable, he taught sutras presenting the view of Mind-Only (*Chittamātra*). He set forth the Vehicle of Solitary Realisers which could help even more persons, and again, to help even more, he set forth the Hearer Vehicle, and within that there are vows for monks, nuns, novices, and two types of vows for lay persons. Within the lowest type of lay person's vow there is assumption of all five precepts or four or three or two or

20

just one, or even just maintaining refuge; there are many who can do this.

Buddha set forth, in accordance with the dispositions and interests of those who could not practise the most profound aspects of his path, limitless forms of stages beginning from a lay person's vow of refuge and going through to training in the Vajra Vehicle of Highest Yoga Tantra. From the viewpoint of number of reasons, vastness, and depth, Buddhism has the most paths and techniques for the transformation of the mind into ultimate goodness.

In order to enter the profound vehicle of Secret Mantra one must know the essentials of the Vajra Vehicle, and for this reason Tsong-ka-pa explains the stages of its path. Among the eighteen volumes of his collected works, the *Great Exposition of the Stages of the Path Common to the Vehicles* and the *Great Exposition of Secret Mantra* are the most important. Many of his books are about selected topics in tantra—the stage of generation, the stage of completion, granting initiation, achieving special activities and so forth—but that which presents in an ordered fashion the important essentials of all four tantras is his *Great Exposition of Secret Mantra* [the first section of which comprises Part Two of this volume].

When an oral transmission explaining the *Great Exposition of Secret Mantra* is given, listeners should have the initiations to the four tantras—for instance, of Mahakarunika for Action Tantra, of Vairochana for Performance Tantra, of Sarvavid for Yoga Tantra, and of Samvara, Guhyasamaja, or Bhairava in a mandala of coloured powders for Highest Yoga Tantra. At the least, one should have an initiation of Highest Yoga Tantra in a mandala of coloured powders or painted cloth. Also, when an oral transmission is bestowed, the lamas who have formed the continuum of the lineage should be identified.

21

The Title

The full title of the *Great Exposition of Secret Mantra* is *The Stages of the Path to a Conqueror and Pervasive Master, a Great Vajradhara: Revealing All Secret Topics*. It indicates the contents of the book. 'Conqueror' generally means one who has conquered over coarse and subtle demons, and on this occasion of Mantra 'Conqueror' refers to conquest over mistaken dualistic appearance. Extremely subtle obstructions to omniscience [which is the simultaneous and direct knowledge of all phenomena and their mode of being] are mentioned only in the teaching of Highest Yoga Tantra, the fourth and highest mantra path. These are the stains of mistaken dualistic appearance that are called appearance, increase, and near attainment. One who has conquered such sources of error by means of their antidotes is a Conqueror. Such a being has completely overcome the coarse and subtle obstructions both to liberation and to omniscience in his own continuum and is also capable of causing the conquest of these obstructions in other sentient beings, thereby overcoming the causes of suffering by which they are stricken.

A Conqueror is 'pervasive' in that the emanator of all Buddha lineages, the Original Protector, Vajradhara, pervades all the lineages, such as those of Vairochana, Akshobhya, Ratnasambhava, Amitabha, and Amoghasiddha. The excellent hundred, five, and three lineages are all included into one basis of emanation, the Body of Enjoyment, the great secret Vajradhara, who is therefore called the 'Master'. Because he pervades and is the master of all lineages, Vajradhara is the 'Pervasive Master'.

A 'vajra' is the best of stones, a diamond; there are external symbolic vajras, as in the case of the vajra and bell used in ritual, and there are vajras that are the meanings symbolised. With respect to the latter, a vajra common to all four sets of tantras is an undifferentiability in one entity of method and wisdom. Method is observation of the vast—the body of a deity—conjoined with an altruistic aspiration to highest enlightenment. Wisdom is the knowledge of the suchness of phenomena just as it is. Also, according only to Highest Yoga Tantra, a vajra is the undifferentiability in one entity of method—great bliss—and wisdom—realisation of emptiness. Because of bearing (*dhara*) such a vajra in his continuum, he is called 'Vajradhara'. He is 'great' because there is none higher. Tsong-ka-pa's text is a presentation of the paths leading to the state of a great Vajradhara, not of assorted essentials of the path in unrelated groups but an arrangement in the order of practice. Since these essentials must be practised in secret, hidden from persons who are not suited for them at this point, these are called the secret topics of the Secret Mantra Vehicle.

Tsong-ka-pa gave this title to his book because it accurately presents in summary, through citing reasoning and scripture, the stages of the path by which one progresses to the ground of a great Vajradhara, pervasive master over all lineages.

The Homage

At the beginning Tsong-ka-pa pays homage in general to his vajra lamas—the chief of whom was Kay-drup-kyung-po-hlay-pa (mKhas-grub-khyung-po-lhas-pa)—and in particular to the revered Manjushri in dependence on whose kindness he realised the essentials of sutra and tantra. The Sanskrit word for homage etymologically means 'seeking the indestructible' and involves physical, verbal, and mental activities; it means, 'I am placing my hope in you'. He pays homage over his continuum of lives to the compassionate lamas who know the essentials of the path and then to his special guru, Manjushri.

23

Because Manjushri is the natural form of the wisdom of all Conquerors, one relies on him as one's special deity in order to increase the wisdom discriminating the truth. Discriminating wisdom thereby increases as it otherwise would not. Tsong-ka-pa and Manjushri met directly, like two people. Originally, Tsong-ka-pa meditated at Ga-wa-dong (dGa'-ba-gdong) in central Tibet in order to achieve a meeting with Manjushri. At Ga-wa-dong there was a Kam-pa (Khams-pa) lama named U-ma-pa Pa-wo-dor-jay (dbU-ma-pa dPa'-bo-rdo-rje) who had been under Manjushri's care for many lifetimes and who had repeated Manjushri's mantra, *oṃ a ra pa tsa na di*, even in his mother's womb. He had been born into a poor shepherd family, and one day when he was out herding sheep he encountered a black Manjushri, after which his intelligence increased. When Tsong-ka-pa met Lama U-ma-pa at Ga-wa-dong, he was able to ask Manjushri questions about the profound emptiness and the vast deeds of compassion of sutra and tantra through Lama U-ma-pa.

There was a painting of Manjushri on the wall of Tsong-ka-pa's Ga-wa-dong retreat, and upon improvement of his meditation a great light emitted from Manjushri's heart. That was the first time Tsong-ka-pa saw Manjushri, and thereafter at his wish he met with Manjushri, who taught him the difficult points of the stages of the path. Therefore, Tsong-ka-pa pays homage to the lowest part of Manjushri's body, his feet.

In ordinary refuge, once our temporary purpose has been satisfied, we no longer need a source of refuge. Here, Tsong-ka-pa takes refuge not for a trifling superficial purpose, but for the ultimate purpose of attaining the fruit of complete liberation from suffering and the causes of suffering, and, since this is not usually done in a few years or even in one lifetime, he pays respectful homage in all his lifetimes. This indicates that the path must be practised within the context of refuge from lifetime to lifetime until becoming a Buddha.

The Expression of Worship

Books are generally divided into three parts, expression of worship, body of the text, and conclusion. Having paid homage to his lamas in general and Manjushri in particular, Tsong-ka-pa begins the expression of worship to spiritual guides. Usually expressions of worship are made to Buddhas and Bodhisattvas; however, Chandrakirti took compassion as his object of worship in his *Supplement to the Middle Way (Madhyamakāvatāra)*, and Maitreya took the Mother, the perfection of wisdom, as the object of worship in his *Ornament for the Realisations (Abhisamayālaṃkāra)*. Here, Tsong-ka-pa takes the lamas as his object of worship. This is because it is necessary to depend on a lama (*guru*) in order to complete the progression through the grounds and paths, and in particular it is extremely important to rely on a qualified spiritual guide in order to train in the paths of Mantra. If one relies on a lama over a long period of time with a union of faith and respect, one can learn quickly and easily the paths that are free from error and from the taints of seeking only one's own welfare. The spiritual guides teach out of great compassion, not out of desire for fame or wealth; they teach without confusion exactly as those paths were taught by Buddha.

Tsong-ka-pa next praises and pays homage to Vajradhara, the Original Protector. Vajradhara, without stirring from the state of the expanse of suchness, which is the extinguishment of all conceptual and dualistic elaborations, appears through his physical sport like a rainbow, emanating collections of deities to countless lands, pure and impure, in many forms, whatever is suitable for taming trainees. A Buddha's Truth Body has

25

two aspects, a Wisdom Truth Body and a Nature Truth Body. Vajradhara's mind, the original innate wisdom, is the Wisdom Truth Body, remaining continuously in meditative equipoise on the expanse of suchness as long as space exists. The final expanse of suchness, the state of extinguishment of all elaborations—both naturally pure and purified of adventitious stains—is the Nature Truth Body.

A Bodhisattva generates a wish to attain Buddhahood for the good of others; therefore, the purpose of actualising the Truth Body is the welfare of others. However, that which directly appears to trainees is not the Truth Body but Form Bodies; thus, it is necessary to help migrators by way of Form Bodies, which a Buddha emanates without stirring from the non-conceptual, non-dualistic Truth Body and without exertion, effort, or thought. Form Bodies appear spontaneously in accordance with the need of trainees.

The subtler of Form Bodies is the Body of Complete Enjoyment, and the coarser are Emanation Bodies, among which there are physically obstructive and non-obstructive types. Thus, this expression of worship indicates the Three Bodies: Truth Body, Complete Enjoyment Body, and Emanation Body, or Four Bodies: Nature Body, Wisdom Body, Complete Enjoyment Body, and Emanation Body. According to Highest Yoga Tantra, the Nature Body can also be considered a product and not necessarily a non-product, as it is considered in the sutra systems, because the clear light wisdom of great bliss that is a Wisdom Truth Body is also said to be a Nature Body. The Complete Enjoyment Body is the sport of mere wind and mind. Emanation Bodies appear in countless pure and impure lands, sometimes with a coarse form. Tsong-ka-pa praises and makes an expression of worship to such a Vajradhara, the lord or principal of the mandalas.

He next makes obeisance to Vajrapani, master of the

secret, leader of the bearers of knowledge mantras, and caretaker of the tantras. Vajrapani collected all the secret essentials, the many and various teachings that Vajradhara set forth from the viewpoint of his exact knowledge of the trainees' disposition, interest, and potential. Tsong-ka-pa pays homage to Vajrapani, arousing his compassion and suggesting that inner and outer demons beware.

Then Tsong-ka-pa takes Manjushri, who is the mother, father, and son of all Conquerors, as a special object of worship. He is the mother of all Conquerors in that he is the essence of all wisdoms; the father of all Conquerors in that he takes the form of spiritual guides and causes beings to generate an altruistic aspiration to highest enlightenment; and the son of all Conquerors in that he assumes the form of Bodhisattvas as he did within Shakyamuni Buddha's retinue.

When a trainee pleases him, Manjushri can, with merely a glance, bestow the wisdom discriminating the truth in the sense of quickly increasing realisation, like lighting a flame. Tsong-ka-pa says that having heard such a marvellous account, he has relied on Manjushri as his special deity over a long time and will not forsake him in the future, there not being another refuge for him. Tsong-ka-pa pays homage to Manjushri as a treasure of wisdom, arousing his compassion through praise and asking him to bestow the fruition of his wishes.

Promise of Composition

At the request especially of Kyap-chok-pel-sang (sKyabs-mchog-dpal-bzang) and Sö-nam-sang-po (bSod-nams-bzang-po), Tsong-ka-pa promises to compose the text for the reasons described above. To do this, he arouses the compassion of the Field-Born, Innate, and Mantra-Born Sky-Goers for the sake of bestowing feats on him, like a mother to her child. Field-Born Sky-Goers are

27

born with bodies of flesh and blood; Innate Sky-Goers have attained realisation of the stage of completion in Highest Yoga Tantra; Mantra-Born Sky-Goers have not yet generated the stage of completion but are abiding in realisation of the stage of generation. According to another interpretation, Field-Born Sky-Goers have attained the subjective clear light [the third of five levels in the stage of completion]; the Innate have lesser realisation but are still within the stage of completion; and Mantra-Born Sky-Goers are said to abide on the stage of generation. Tsong-ka-pa requests these feminine caretakers of tantra to be affectionate to him and overcome all obstacles to clear presentation of tantric doctrine and, seeing the purpose of his deeds, to grant the feats and activities benefiting all beings.

Refuge

We live in an ocean of cyclic existence whose depth and extent cannot be measured. We are troubled again and again by the afflictions of desire and hatred as if repeatedly attacked by sharks.

Our mental and physical aggregates are impelled by former contaminated actions and afflictions and serve as a basis for present suffering as well as inducing future suffering. While such cyclic existence lasts, we have various thoughts of pleasure and displeasure: 'If I do this, what will people think? If I do not do this, I will be too late; I won't make any profit.' When we see something pleasant we think, 'Oh, if I could only have that!' We see that others are prosperous, and we generate jealousy, unable to bear their prosperity. We see an attractive man or woman, and we want a relationship. We are not satisfied with a passing relationship but want it to last forever. And then, once staying together with that person, we desire someone else. When we see someone we do not like, we become angry and quarrel after a single word; we feel we cannot remain even for an hour near this hated person but must leave immediately. Day and night, night and day we spend our lives in the company of the afflictions, generating desire for the pleasant and anger at the unpleasant, and continue thus even when dreaming, unable to remain relaxed, our minds completely and utterly mixed with thoughts of desire and hatred without interruption.

To what refuge should we go? A source of refuge must have completely overcome all defects forever; it must be free of all faults. It must also have all the attributes of altruism—those attainments which are necessary for achieving others' welfare. For it is doubtful that anyone

29

lacking these two prerequisites can bestow refuge; it would be like falling into a ditch and asking another who is in it to help you out. You need to ask someone who is standing outside the ditch for help; it is senseless to ask another who is in the same predicament. A refuge capable of protecting from the frights of manifold sufferings cannot also be bound in this suffering but must be free and unflawed. Furthermore, the complete attainments are necessary, for if you have fallen into a ditch, it is useless to seek help from someone standing outside it who does not wish to help or who wishes to help but has no means to do so.

Only a Buddha has extinguished all faults and gained all attainments. Therefore, one should mentally go for refuge to a Buddha, praise him with speech, and respect him physically. One should enter the teaching of such a being.

A Buddha's abandonment of defects is of three types: good, complete, and irreversible. Good abandonment involves overcoming obstructions through their antidotes, not just through withdrawing from those activities. Complete abandonment is not trifling, forsaking only some afflictions or just the manifest afflictions, but forsaking all obstructions. Irreversible abandonment overcomes the seeds of afflictions and other obstructions in such a way that defects will never arise again, even when conditions favourable to them are present.

Tsong-ka-pa's intention in praising Buddhism is not to insult other teachers such as Kapila. Statements of the greatness of Buddhism are made in order to develop one-pointedness of mind toward practice, for one who is able to practise Buddhism must generate effort to do so. It is necessary for him to have confidence in Buddha's teaching from the round orb of his heart. There is a Tibetan saying that one cannot sew with a two-pointed needle or achieve aims with a two-pointed mind. Similarly, if a practitioner is hesitant, he will not put great force into the practice of any one system. Tsong-ka-pa states that Buddhism is the best in order that persons who would be helped more through engaging in the Buddhist path than through another system might not be diverted to another path.

Mere belief in a source of refuge is not firm; unless there is valid cognition, you are going only on the assertion that Buddhism is good. Refuge is not an act of partisanship but is based on analysing what scriptures are reasonable and what scriptures are not. In order for the mind to engage one-pointedly in practice, there must be reasoned conviction that only the Buddhist path is non-mistaken and capable of leading to the state of complete freedom from defects and possession of all auspicious attainments. One should engage in honest investigation, avoiding desire and hatred and seeking the teaching that sets forth the means for fulfilling the aims of trainees.

The fruit of practice is the achievement of two types of aims: the temporary fruit of high status and the final fruit of definite goodness. High status refers to a life as a human or a god rather than as an animal, a hungry ghost, or a hell-being. Definite goodness is complete liberation from cyclic existence and the attainment of a Buddha's omniscience. Buddhism has teachings based on each as well as their means of achievement. High status is achieved first, and definite goodness is achieved later because it depends on the former; however, the validity of scriptures with respect to achieving definite goodness should be proven first. When the validity of scriptures presenting liberation and the means to achieve it has been proved with reasoning and when the conviction of valid cognition has arisen, it is possible to gain conviction with respect to the incontrovertibility of scriptures that teach high status and its means.

Buddha's teachings on non-manifest phenomena, such as the extremely subtle presentations of actions and their effects—which are very hidden phenomena—cannot be proved with reasoning. How then can they be verified?

There is no need to verify manifest phenomena through reasoning because they appear directly to the senses. The slightly hidden, however, can be proved with reasoning that generates inferential understanding, and since emptiness is very profound but only slightly hidden, it is accessible to reasoning. Then, when conviction is generated in the incontrovertibility of his teaching on the very profound emptiness, conviction is gained in the validity of Buddha's teachings on very hidden phenomena that are not accessible to reasoning but are not so important.

For instance, with respect to accounts of the effects of actions that Buddha gives in sutras such as the *Wise Man and the Fool (Damamūkonāmasūtra)*, we may wonder how it could possibly be so. Since these are very hidden phenomena, they cannot be proved with reasoning, and it seems that Buddha can say whatever he likes. However, through our own experience we can confirm Buddha's teachings on more important topics such as emptiness, the altruistic mind of enlightenment, love, and compassion, for no matter who analyses—Buddhist or non-Buddhist —or how much one analyses, if the person is not biased through desire or hatred, these teachings can bear analysis and serve as powerful sources of thought. When you see that Buddha does not err with regard to these more important phenomena, you can for the first time accept his other presentations.

Some wrongly think that the afflicted phenomena of cyclic existence and the purified phenomena of nirvana cannot be proved by reasoning and that since liberation and omniscience cannot be directly seen, and are not manifest, they can be proved only through citation of scripture. They believe only in scripture and are displaying their own lack of foundation. Such a statement of refuge is only a proclamation of the weakness of that refuge. The process of cyclic existence and the eradication of it can be proved by the reasoning that establishes the misconception of inherent existence as its root cause and establishes the wisdom cognising emptiness as its antidote.

Even scriptures that present very hidden phenomena, inaccessible to both direct perception and inference, are proved to be valid through three modes of analysis. The three modes are establishment (1) that the passage is not damaged by direct valid cognition in its teaching of manifest phenomena, (2) that the passage is not damaged by evidential inference in its teaching of slightly hidden phenomena and (3) that the passage is not damaged by scriptural inference in its teaching of very hidden phenomena in the sense of containing internal contradictions and so forth. Thus, even this process derives from reasoning.

Buddhist scriptures do not have inner contradictions whereas non-Buddhist scriptures do. This is not to say that non-Buddhist scriptures will not be valid with respect to certain meanings, but they do have contradictions with respect to the phenomena included within the afflicted realm and with respect to phenomena included within the realm of purification. The Forders' scriptures have non-mistaken explanations of how to generate the four concentrations and the four formless absorptions as well as small achievements of altruism. However, with respect to the chief aims of persons, their scriptures contain inner contradictions. For example, they assert that the creator of the world is permanent and then assert that the cyclic existence created by this permanent creator can be overcome. If the cause were permanent, the effect would have to remain permanent. However, since the effect is impermanent, the cause must be impermanent. It is the nature of things that if the cause is not overcome, the effect cannot be overcome; thus, there could not be an end to cyclic existence. As Dharmakirti says:

> Because the permanent cannot be overcome
> It is impossible to overcome its force.

It is necessary first to prove that the root of cyclic existence is the conception of self—the conception of inherent existence. Then it can be shown that a system asserting a view of self and thereby rejecting the view of selflessness would be self-contradictory when it asserts the attainment of liberation from cyclic existence.

This implies that from the viewpoint of the highest Buddhist philosophical system, Prasangika-Madhyamika, the views of the lower systems—Svatantrika, Chittamatra, Sautrantika, and Vaibhashika—also seem to contain inner contradictions. According to the Prasangika-Madhyamika system, the root of cyclic existence is the conception of the inherent existence of phenomena and the consequent misconception of the inherent existence of the 'I', called the view of the transitory collection as a real 'I'. The other Buddhist systems assert an inherent existence of phenomena whereas the Prasangikas assert that inherent existence is the referent object of a mistaken consciousness conceiving self. Thus, the lower schools' assertion of liberation from cyclic existence involves a seeming inner contradiction which is resolved only through considering this teaching a non-final doctrine given to those who could not comprehend the highest view.

The path of liberation removes the adventitious defilements from the expanse of suchness which itself is intrinsically pure, and liberation is the state in which these adventitious defilements have been removed. It seems that some teachers did not know this liberation or the path to it and set forth systems in ignorance. The *Kalachakra*

Tantra (Kālachakra), after setting forth the various systems of Buddhist and non-Buddhist tenets and presenting with reasoning their relative superiority and inferiority, says, 'It is not suitable to despise another system.' The reason given is that often non-Buddhist systems have been taught through the empowering blessings of Buddhas.

There are cases of teachers' explaining paths in ignorance, but other teachers were emanations of Buddhas, free from all defects and endowed with all attainments. They knew the difference between the mistaken and non-mistaken paths, but because at that point there was no purpose in teaching the non-mistaken path, they set forth a non-final path, pretending not to know another.

One who has the ability should proceed on the non-mistaken path; however, in relation to one for whom another path is suitable, that path is right. For instance, for a person who can practise the Chittamatra view but not the Madhyamika view, the Chittamatra view is unmistaken. The same is also true with regard to non-Buddhist teachings. Therefore, other teachers, their doctrines, and practitioners can be refuges, but not final refuges.

When conviction in the sources of refuge is generated through unbiased investigation and proper reasoning, faith is firm and powerful. Such faith cannot be generated in reliance on scripture alone. The means for generating such conviction are set forth in Dharmakirti's *Seven Treatises*—three main works and four works of elaboration. Of the three main works, the extensive one is his *Commentary on (Dignaga's) 'Compendium of Valid Cognition' (Pramāṇavarttika)*; the middling is his *Ascertainment of Valid Cognition (Pramāṇavinishchaya)*, and the condensed is his *Drop of Reasoning (Nyāyabindu)*. The four works of elaboration are his *Drop of Reasons (Hetubindu), Analysis of Relations (Saṃba-*

ndhaparīkṣhā), Reasoning for Debate (Vādanyāya),
and *Proof of Other Continuums (Saṃtānāntarasiddhi).*
Inner conviction arises from reasoned investigation.

Hinayana and Mahayana

A Hearer's mode of practice accords with that of the Hinayana discipline, one-pointedly viewing the desire realm attributes of pleasant forms, sounds, odours, tastes, and tangible objects as faulty. Aryadeva says that those who engage in this practice which is free from desire have 'an interest in the lowly' because this path accords with the nature of a mind lacking the strength of the unusual attitude that bears the burden of all sentient beings' welfare. Since they are unable to practise using the great power of desire in the path, they are taught a mode free from desire.

As long as you cannot use desire in the path there is a danger of coming under its influence, in which case it is better to proceed only on a path that is free from desire. Otherwise, if you attempt to use desire in the path you will be harmed instead of helped. Prohibition is the only course. This is the mode of Hinayana practice.

For those having an interest in the vast, the Sutra Mahayana practices of the grounds and the perfections are taught; these comprise the causal Perfection Vehicle. Those who, in addition to having an interest in the vast, have a special interest in the ultimate profundity, are taught practices wherein desire is used in the path. This is Tantra Mahayana.

The Indian scholar Tripitakamala also includes all Buddha's teaching into these three modes, the Hinayana mode of the four noble truths, the Sutra Mahayana mode of the perfections—giving, ethics, patience, effort, concentration, and wisdom—and the Tantra Mahayana mode of Secret Mantra. Thus, Buddha's word is divided into the two scriptural divisions of Hinayana and Mahayana, and the vehicles or paths that are the subjects of expression by Buddha's word are also divided into the two, Hinayana and Mahayana.

Hinayana is further divided into two vehicles, Hearer Vehicle *(Shrāvakayāna)* and Solitary Realiser Vehicle *(Pratyekabuddhayāna)*. Solitary Realisers are of two types, congregating and rhinoceros-like. Congregating Solitary Realisers are a little more social, staying in a group or community for a longer period than the rhinoceros-like, who find it unsuitable to stay in society and live alone. Hearers and Solitary Realisers equally abandon the conception of inherent existence, but Solitary Realisers amass more merit than Hearers and thus, when they actualise the fruit of their vehicle, are capable of becoming Foe Destroyers—destroyers of the foe, the afflictions, the principal of which is the conception of inherent existence—without depending on a teacher in that lifetime. They actualise the fruit of their vehicle 'independently' through the force of accumulating merit for a hundred aeons. Solitary Realisers are said to be very proud and independent-minded. They mostly attain their enlightenment in a dark age when no Buddhas appear—perhaps so that they will not be outshone by a Buddha's presence but more likely in order to be of greater benefit to others. As Nagarjuna says in his *Treatise on the Middle Way* (*Madhyamakashāstra*, XVIII.12):

> Though the perfect Buddhas do not appear
> And Hearers have disappeared,
> A Solitary Realiser's wisdom
> Arises without support.

Both Hearers and Solitary Realisers seek the wisdom cognising the non-inherent existence of all phenomena —persons and other phenomena. This is because the chief fetter binding one in cyclic existence is the conception of inherent existence, the other fetters being the afflictions such as desire, hatred and ignorance that depend on the conception of inherent existence. According to Mantra, the causes binding one in cyclic existence are two, ignorance and winds [currents of energy] and among them the chief is the ignorance conceiving inherent existence. The winds that serve as the mount of afflicted conceptual thought are co-operative causes in the process of cyclic existence.

Hearers and Solitary Realisers understand that without the wisdom cognising selflessness it is impossible to overcome cyclic existence. They understand that they need this wisdom and seek it in company with ethics, meditative stabilisation, and so forth. Through this path all afflictions are extinguished.

There are four schools of Buddhist tenets—Vaibhashika, Sautrantika, Chittamatra, and Madhyamika; the highest of these is Madhyamika which is further divided into Svatantrika-Madhyamika and Prasangika-Madhyamika. Prasangika-Madhyamika is considered to be the highest philosophical view, its teachers having been Nagarjuna, Aryadeva, Buddhapalita, Chandrakirti, Shantideva, Atisha, and so forth. According to the Prasangika system, Hinayanists—those who are unable to bear the burden of all sentient beings' welfare but seek only their own liberation from cyclic existence—and Mahayanists—those able to bear the burden of the welfare of all sentient beings throughout space—equally cognise the subtle emptiness of both persons and other phenomena. They realise that both persons and other phenomena, such as mind and body, do not inherently exist, or exist in their own right.

However, the non-Prasangika schools all say that Hinayanists—Hearers and Solitary Realisers—cognise only a selflessness of persons which is a person's non-substantial existence in the sense that a person does

39

not have a character different from the character of mind and body. From the Prasangika viewpoint, however, this wisdom is not sufficient as a means of liberation from cyclic existence, and furthermore, the other schools have described not the innate form of the misconception of persons as substantially existent entities, but the artificial. According to the Prasangikas, the innate form of this coarse misconception of self is the apprehension of a person as controller of mind and body, like a master over his servants, but it does not involve an apprehension of the person as having a character different from mind and body. Apprehension of a person as having a character different from mind and body occurs only through the intellectual acquisition of tenets of non-Buddhist systems and thus is called 'artificial', not 'innate'. From the viewpoint of the Prasangika-Madhyamika system, the selflessness of persons that is set forth by the lower schools is thus only a *coarse* selflessness and is merely the negative of self as misconceived by an *artificial* misconception of the nature of a person.

The non-Prasangika systems—Svatantrika, Chittamatra, Sautrantika, and Vaibhashika—assert that Hearers and Solitary Realisers do not cognise a selflessness of phenomena other than persons; they cognise only the selflessness of persons—that the person is empty of substantial existence, or self-sufficiency. They assert that merely through this Hearers and Solitary Realisers attain liberation. Tsong-ka-pa's position is clear that according to the non-Prasangika systems Hearers and Solitary Realisers attain liberation in this way. When he describes the type of selflessness that they cognise, he says that they do not cognise that the person is empty of natural existence but cognise that the person is empty of a substantial existence *as is imputed by the non-Buddhists.* He seems to be saying that according to the Vaibhashika and Sautrantika systems of tenets themselves, one need only cognise that a person is empty of being a permanent, partless, independent entity. However, we have to say that the Svatantrikas, Chittamatrins, Sautrantikas, and Vaibhashikas do not assert that cognition of a person's emptiness of being permanent, partless, and independent opposes the *innate* misconception of self. In their own systems the conception of the person as permanent, partless, and independent is only artificial, intellectually acquired, not innate.

The innate misconception of self—not involving reasoned affirmation—binds beings in cyclic existence, and according to these systems it is the conception that a person is a substantially existent or self-sufficient entity. The non-Prasangika systems themselves say that no matter how much one meditates on a person's not being permanent, partless, and independent, this cannot harm the conception of substantial existence or self-sufficiency. Therefore, according to them, Hearers and Solitary Realisers cognise a selflessness which is the person's non-substantial or non-self-sufficient nature. They must train in such a path and proceed by this means.

Tsong-ka-pa here and in other places seems to say that in the lower systems themselves the subtle selflessness of the person is described as a person's not being permanent, partless, and independent. Many scholars say that Tsong-ka-pa's reference is to the implications of the lower systems as seen from the Prasangika viewpoint. This means that when Prasangikas consider the reasons proving selflessness that are set forth in the lower systems, they find that the inherent or natural existence of the person is taken for granted and that their reasoning for refuting self has the ability only to refute the existence of a person that has a character different from the character of mind and body.

According to the Prasangika system, if one does not cognise the non-inherent existence of the person, one

41

cannot eliminate the conception of a self of persons. If the conception of inherent existence with regard to the mental and physical aggregates is not overcome, the conception of the inherent existence of the person cannot be overcome. Cyclic existence is achieved through the power of actions, and actions are achieved through the power of afflictions. Since this is so, ceasing actions meets back to ceasing afflictions. Ceasing afflictions, in turn, meets back to ceasing conceptions. Ceasing conceptions meets back to ceasing the elaborations of the conception of inherent existence which are ceased only by a mind cognising emptiness.

According to the final thought of the *Perfection of Wisdom Sutras*, liberation from cyclic existence definitely involves cognition of the selflessness of both persons and other phenomena. This is taught not only in the Mahayana but also in the Hinayana scriptures, though not in the Hinayana systems, Vaibhashika and Sautrantika. However, various ways of proceeding on the path are presented in the scriptures of both vehicles, and these must be distinguished to determine which require interpretation and which are definitive. For instance, it is taught that merely through cognising the coarse selflessness—the person's lack of substantial or self-sufficient existence—liberation can be attained whereas this cognition, as well as that of impermanence, can only train the mental continuum, not liberate it.

In general, we are under the strong influence of the conception of inherent existence, and due to it we do not wish to be liberated from cyclic existence. However, when we see that all products are impermanent, this helps to advance us to the point where we can overcome the conception of inherent existence. Those who are vessels only for such paths, training the mental continuum but not liberating it, are trainees of dull faculties. Those who are also vessels for the path of liberation are suitable for the teaching of the selflessness of phenomena. Thus, among Hinayana trainees there are two types, dull and sharp, the latter being the main or special trainees of Hinayana, but not the majority.

The mother, the perfection of wisdom, is the common cause of all four sons, Hearer, Solitary Realiser, Bodhisattva, and Buddha Superiors; thus, Hinayana and Mahayana are not differentiated by way of view but by way of accompanying methods. In particular, these are the aspirational and practical minds of enlightenment and the deeds of the six perfections, found in Mahayana but not in Hinayana.

'Vehicle' *(yāna)* has two meanings: the means by which one progresses and the destination to which one is progressing. Mahayana in the sense of the vehicle by which one progresses means to be motivated by the mind of enlightenment—wishing to attain highest enlightenment for the sake of all sentient beings, one's objects of intent—and means to engage in the six perfections. These paths of training are the paths of Mahayana in general, and even though Madhyamika and Chittamatra have different views, these two are not different vehicles because the vehicles are differentiated by way of method and the method—the altruistic mind of enlightenment and its attendant practices—is the same in Chittamatra and Madhyamika. Still, those who are able to penetrate the subtle selflessness of phenomena, as presented in Madhyamika, are the main trainees of Mahayana. The Mantra division of Mahayana, including all four sets of tantras, has exactly the same motivation—altruistic mind generation—and deeds—the six perfections.

Seeing reason and need, Buddha set forth many systems and vehicles, but these did not arise due to his being intimate with some and alien to others. The trainees who were listening to his teaching had various dispositions, interests, and abilities, and thus he taught methods that

43

were suitable for each of them. For those who temporarily did not have the courage to strive for Buddhahood or who did not at all have the capacity of obtaining Buddhahood at that time, Buddha did not say, 'You can attain Buddhahood.' Rather, he set forth a path appropriate to the trainees' abilities. Buddha spoke in terms of their situation, and everything that he spoke was a means of eventually attaining highest enlightenment even though he did not always say that these were means for attaining Buddhahood.

Since the purpose of a Buddha's coming is others' realisation of the wisdom of Buddhahood, the methods for actualising this wisdom are one vehicle, not two. A Buddha does not lead beings by a vehicle that does not proceed to Buddhahood; he establishes beings in his own level. A variety of vehicles is set forth in accordance with temporary needs.

Question: Maitreya has taught that if someone bearing the Mahayana lineage came temporarily to abide in a hell, this would not interrupt his progress to stainless enlightenment. However, if he were attracted to Hinayana practices, leading solely to peace, seeking to bring help and happiness only to himself, this would greatly interrupt his progress to Buddhahood. Thus, according to Maitreya, generating a Hinayana attitude is a greater obstacle than taking birth in a hell; so, how can it be said that Hinayana is a means leading to Buddhahood?

Answer: If one who has the ability to practise Mahayana does not practise it, and instead assumes Hinayana practices, this action will interrupt his progress to Buddhahood. It is not said that with respect to all people generation of a Hinayana attitude is an obstacle to Buddhahood. It is so only for those capable of practicing the Bodhisattva path. It depends on the individual.

Nevertheless, Hinayana is not part of Mahayana. Hinayana paths are subsidiaries of the path to Buddhahood but not actual Mahayana paths. Mahayana has the complete paths for the attainment of Buddhahood; thus, there is a difference of incompleteness and completeness, and hence inferiority and superiority, between Hinayana and Mahayana. Hinayana is a separate but not final vehicle because everyone has the Buddha nature that makes full enlightenment possible.

The teaching that the Buddha nature is present in all sentient beings, providing the 'substantial cause' for the attainment of Buddhahood, inspires courage. This is the Buddha lineage of which there are two types, natural and transformational. The natural Buddha lineage is the emptiness of the mind, and, according to Mantra, the transformational Buddha lineage is the defiled mind of clear light which serves as the cause of Buddhahood.

In the Nyingma school of the earlier translations, it is said that Buddhahood exists primordially in oneself. This teaching refers to the very subtle mind of clear light that we presently have in our continuum; it is not different from the mind of a Buddha in terms of the entity of the basic innate mind. The continuum of our basic innate mind will become a Buddha's Wisdom Body; therefore, we presently have all the substances for achieving Buddhahood, and we should not seek for Buddhahood elsewhere. This is a very famous and meaningful precept in the religious language of the Nyingma order.

If we think of the Buddha nature merely in terms of an emptiness of inherent existence, it is not so meaningful, for then it could be said that a pot's emptiness would be a Buddha nature because it is an emptiness of inherent existence. Here in this Nyingma teaching there is the strong suggestion that a positive phenomenon—the mind of clear light—is the Buddha nature.

Since the substances that make enlightenment possible

45

are present in all sentient beings' continuums and since a Buddha knows the means of leading all these trainees through the stages of the path, if he hid that means from them, he would have the fault of miserliness. His mind would be biased. His compassion would not be unimpeded. On the contrary, the various vehicles that Buddha taught out of his unlimited compassion are all methods for achieving omniscience.

Shantideva's *Engaging in the Bodhisattva Deeds (Bodhisattvacharyāvatāra)* says that the truthful Buddha taught that even bees and donkeys can attain Buddhahood if they generate effort. Therefore, since we now have attained a human body and have met with the doctrine, if we generate the power of courageous effort, why could we not attain Buddhahood?

Vajrayana

The Secret Mantra Vehicle is hidden because it is not appropriate for the minds of many persons. Practices for achieving activities of pacification, increase, control and fierceness, which are not even presented in the Perfection Vehicle, are taught in the Mantra Vehicle but in hiding because those with impure motivation would harm both themselves and others by engaging in them. If one's mental continuum has not been ripened by the practices common to both Sutra and Tantra Mahayana—realisation of suffering, impermanence, refuge, love, compassion, altruistic mind generation, and emptiness of inherent existence—practice of the Mantra Vehicle can be ruinous through one's assuming an advanced practice inappropriate to one's capacity. Therefore, its open dissemination is prohibited; practitioners must maintain secrecy from those who are not vessels of this path.

The word 'mantra' means 'mind-protection'. It protects the mind from ordinary appearances and conceptions. 'Mind' here refers to all six consciousnesses—eye, ear, nose, tongue, body and mental consciousnesses—which are to be freed, or protected, from the ordinary world. There are two factors in mantra training, pride in oneself as a deity and vivid appearance of that deity. Divine pride protects one from the pride of being ordinary, and divine vivid appearance protects one from ordinary appearances. Whatever appears to the senses is viewed as the sport of a deity; for instance, whatever forms are seen are viewed as the emanations of a deity and whatever sounds are heard are viewed as the mantras of a deity. One is thereby protected from ordinary appearances, and through this transformation of attitude, the pride of being a deity emerges. Such protection of mind together with its attendant pledges and vows is called the practice of mantra.

In another way, the syllable *man* in 'mantra' is said to be 'knowledge of suchness', and *tra* is etymologised as *trāya*, meaning 'compassion protecting migrators'. This explanation is shared by all four sets of tantras, but from the specific viewpoint of Highest Yoga Tantra, compassion protecting migrators can be considered the wisdom of great bliss. This interpretation is devised in terms of a contextual etymology of the Sanskrit word for 'compassion', *karuṇā*, as 'stopping pleasure'. When anyone generates compassion—the inability to bear sentient beings' suffering without acting to relieve it, pleasure, peacefulness, and relaxation are temporarily stopped. Thus, in Highest Yoga the word 'compassion' (*karuṇā*) is designated to stopping the pleasure of the emission of the vital essence and refers to the wisdom of great bliss (*mahāsukha*). It is the mantra of definitive meaning and the deity of definitive meaning.

'Compassion protecting migrators' can be interpreted in a way common to all four tantras as an undifferentiable union of the wisdom cognising emptiness and great compassion, or a union of wisdom and method—wisdom conjoined with method and method conjoined with wisdom.

'Vehicle' can be considered in two aspects, an effect vehicle—the object to which one is progressing—and a cause vehicle—the means by which one progresses. Even though the Vajra Vehicle has both cause and effect vehicles, it is called the Effect Vehicle because a path of imagination is practised wherein one believingly assumes the aspects of the four thorough purities—the *abode* where a Tathagata resides after full enlightenment, the *body* that is a manifestation of the Wisdom Truth Body in the form of a residence and residents, the *resources* that are enjoyed in the high status of Buddhahood, and the supreme *activities* of a Buddha's ripening sentient beings. Similitudes of these four factors of the effect state are cultivated in meditation.

According to Highest Yoga Tantra the effect—the Mantra mode—is the wisdom of great bliss, and the cause—the Perfection mode—is the wisdom cognising emptiness as presented in the Madhyamika scriptures. The indivisibility of these two is the meaning of 'indivisibility of bliss and emptiness'.

According to the *Kalachakra Tantra*, the cause is emptiness, but this emptiness is not a negation of inherent existence; it is a negation of physical particles. This is called 'form of emptiness', form empty of physical particles, form beyond matter. This form of emptiness, adorned with the major and minor marks of a Buddha in father and mother aspect, is the cause, and the supreme immutable bliss, which is induced in dependence on various empty forms, is the effect. A union of these two is the Cause-Effect Vehicle. Such an indivisibility of the totally supreme form of emptiness and the supreme immutable bliss in the continuum of a learner is a vehicle in the sense of being the means by which one progresses. In the continuum of a non-learner, a Buddha, it is a vehicle in the sense of being that to which one is progressing. Thus, there are two unions of the totally supreme form of emptiness and supreme immutable bliss.

This way of presenting the undifferentiability of method and wisdom is only from the viewpoint of Highest Yoga Tantra, and specifically that of the *Kalachakra Tantra*. Such an explanation does not apply to the three lower tantras—Action, Performance, and Yoga—because they do not have the means of generating the immutable great bliss. *Kalachakra Tantra* has six branches: withdrawal, concentration, vitality and exertion, holding, mindfulness, and meditative stabilisation. During the branch of mindfulness a form of emptiness is achieved, and in dependence on it, supreme immutable bliss is generated—this being the branch of meditative stabilisation. The three lower tantras do not have all the factors included in the first five causal branches and thus, of course, do not have the sixth.

Indivisibility of method and wisdom indicates the necessity of proceeding with an inseparable method and wisdom in order to attain the fruit of definite goodness, which is liberation from cyclic existence as well as omniscience. This mode of progress is common to all vehicles, Cause and Effect. In the Perfection Vehicle 'inseparable method and wisdom' refers to method conjoined with wisdom and wisdom conjoined with method. When the altruistic mind of enlightenment is manifest, the mind actually cognising emptiness is not present, and when an actual cognition of emptiness is manifest, an altruistic mind of enlightenment is not present. According to the Perfection Vehicle, it is unsuitable merely to stay in meditative equipoise on emptiness without also engaging at other times in the perfections of giving and so forth, and it is also unsuitable merely to engage in the practices of giving and so forth without engaging at other times in meditation on emptiness. Since this is the case, a yogi of the Perfection Vehicle must cultivate a mind cognising emptiness and then, within non-diminishment of the force of reflection on all phenomena as a magician's illusions, train in giving, ethics, patience, and so forth. Also, within non-diminishment of the force of his altruistic aspiration, he must train in cognising emptiness. This is the inseparability of method and wisdom in the Perfection Vehicle.

In Mantra it is even deeper. Here, the inseparability of method and wisdom does not mean that wisdom and method are different entities conjoined; rather, method and wisdom are included in one entity. In Mantra these two are complete in the different aspects of one consciousness.

If, as in the *Kalachakra Tantra*, one posited method as the totally supreme form of emptiness and posited wisdom as the supreme immutable bliss, then this would not apply in general to all four tantras. Therefore, what is the meaning of inseparable method and wisdom, or 'Vajra Vehicle', that applies to all four tantras? The six perfections are included in method and wisdom, and in Mantra, method and wisdom are considered as the one entity of the Vajrasattva meditative stabilisation. This is a consciousness taking cognisance of appearance—the body of a deity—and realising its emptiness of inherent existence. The yoga of non-dual profundity and appearance is the Vajrasattva meditative stabilisation. Being an indivisibility of method and wisdom, this is a vajra in the sense of being that to which one is progressing—in the continuum of a non-learner—and in the sense of being the means by which one progresses—in the continuum of a learner.

Because the Mantra Vehicle has more varieties of methods or skilful means than the Perfection Vehicle, it is also called the Method Vehicle. Because the effect itself is taken as the path in the sense that one presently cultivates the four thorough purities—abode, body, resources and activities of the effect state—it is called the Effect Vehicle. Because it must be practised in extreme secrecy, it is called the Secret Vehicle. Because it contains the topics of training of Knowledge Bearers, it is also called the Scriptural Division of the Knowledge Bearers.

The tantras can be considered as a fourth scriptural division beyond the three scriptural divisions of sutra—discipline, sets of discourses, and knowledge—or as included in the three divisions. However, there is good reason to consider them as included in the sets of

51

discourses. From among the three trainings, ethics, meditative stabilisation, and wisdom, the tantras' feature of profundity is mainly concerned with the training in meditative stabilisation. The discipline section of the scriptures mainly teaches the training in ethics; the sets of discourses mainly teach the training in meditative stabilisation; and the knowledge section mainly teaches the training in wisdom. Since the tantras contain extraordinary means for achieving meditative stabilisation, the tantras that express these means can be included in the sets of discourses.

In Tsong-ka-pa's miscellaneous works there is a question concerning this, to which he answers that the difference of profundity in the tantras occurs through meditative stabilisation. There is also a difference with respect to the training in ethics and a small difference with respect to the training in wisdom in terms of the type of consciousness cognising emptiness, but the main difference is found in the meditative stabilisation that is a union of calm abiding and special insight. Let us discuss this.

As presented in the Perfection Vehicle, the achievement of Buddhahood involves at least three countless aeons of practice; the first accumulation of merit over countless aeons occurs on the paths of accumulation and preparation. The second occurs on the first seven Bodhisattva grounds, which are called impure because the conception of inherent existence has not yet been fully abandoned. The third accumulation of merit over countless aeons occurs on the eighth, ninth, and tenth grounds, which are called pure because the conception of inherent existence has been totally abandoned.

The three lower tantras present yoga with signs and yoga without signs which possess a special method for quickly generating a union of calm abiding and special insight that is a wisdom 'arisen from meditation' cognising

52

emptiness. Thereby, the first accumulation of merit over countless aeons is accomplished in a shorter period of time. Then, from the first Bodhisattva ground on through to Buddhahood the three lower tantras present the path much as it is presented in the Perfection Vehicle.

A special trainee of Mantra initially generates an altruistic aspiration to highest enlightenment and then trains in the Mantra paths. For instance, according to Action Tantra, which is the lowest among the four sets of tantras, a yogi engages in such practices as the four-branched repetition and subsequently practises the three concentrations—abiding in fire, abiding in sound, and bestowing liberation at the end of sound. During the concentrations of abiding in fire and abiding in sound, the capacity of meditative stabilisation becomes powerful. Through this, a meditative stabilisation that is a union of calm abiding and special insight is achieved in the course of the concentration that bestows liberation at the end of sound. This is a quicker path for the achievement of calm abiding and special insight than that found in the Perfection Vehicle.

Performance Tantra, the second of the four tantras, also has this distinguishing feature with regard to achieving meditative stabilisation, while Yoga Tantra and Highest Yoga Tantra have even more profound techniques of meditative stabilisation for achieving a union of calm abiding and special insight. Thus, even though there is a difference between the Perfection and Mantra Vehicles with respect to the training in ethics, the outstanding difference occurs with respect to the training in meditative stabilisation.

Clear Light

'Tantra' means 'continuum', like a stream, of which there are three types: base, path, and fruit. The base tantra is the person who is practising. According to the *Guhyasamaja (Guhyasamāja)*, a Highest Yoga Tantra, there are five lineages of persons—white lotus, utpala, lotus, sandalwood, and jewel, the last being the supreme person. The base continuum is also the naturally abiding lineage, the element, the Buddha nature, the Tathagata essence. It is called the base because it is the basis of the activity of the path.

The path tantras are the paths purifying that base. According to the lower tantras, these are the yogas with and without signs and, according to Highest Yoga Tantra, the stages of generation and completion that purify the defilements related with the suchness of the mind.

The fruit tantra is the state of the effect, the Truth Body, complete extinguishment of all defilements as a Vajradhara. The three tantras—base, path, and fruit —contain the subjects and meanings of all sets of tantras, and continuums of words [texts] that express these subjects are called expressional word tantras that are divided into sets or groups.

The Perfection Vehicle is just the training in the altruistic mind of enlightenment and the six perfections; it does not clearly present any other mode of progress on the path. Mantra takes these as its basis but has other distinguishing paths. Since the Mantra Vehicle also has the practice of the altruistic mind of enlightenment and training in the six perfections, Tsong-ka-pa says that the Perfection Vehicle *only* has these paths.

There is no difference between the Perfection and

Mantra Vehicles with regard to the two objects of altruistic mind generation—the field of intent which is the welfare of other sentient beings and the object of observation which is one's own attainment of Buddhahood. Trainees of Sutra and Mantra wish for highest enlightenment for the sake of others and take cognisance of the same fruit, a Buddhahood that is an extinguishment of all faults and an endowment with all auspicious qualities.

There is also no difference in view, for Mantra does not explain a view of the middle way which exceeds that presented in the Perfection Vehicle by Nagarjuna. Even if there were a difference in view, this could not serve to differentiate the two vehicles since Chittamatra and Madhyamika, which have different views, are compatible in one vehicle.

The difference in vehicles must be determined through either wisdom or method. Because the wisdom cognising emptiness is the mother common to all four sons—Hearer, Solitary Realiser, Bodhisattva, and Buddha Superiors —Hinayana and Mahayana are differentiated by way of method, not by way of wisdom. For the same reason, the Perfection and Mantra Vehicles are differentiated by way of method, not wisdom.

Tsong-ka-pa says that there is no difference in view between Hinayana and Mahayana and, within Mahayana, between the Perfection Vehicle and the Mantra Vehicle. He is referring to the 'view' in terms of the object, emptiness—the objective clear light—not in terms of the wisdom consciousness cognising emptiness—the subjective clear light. The Sakya Pandita of the Sakya Order also held that Secret Mantra does not have a view different from the Perfection Vehicle and that if it did, that view would involve dualistic elaborations. Since the Madhyamika view has passed beyond the limits of elaborations, a view different from it would have to involve such.

In the old translation order of Nyingma there is said to be a difference in view between Sutra and Mantra, but this difference is primarily concerned with the subject. Nyingma does not make a clear distinction between the subject—the wisdom consciousness—and the object —emptiness—because on the higher stages of the path, subject and object are mixed undifferentiably in one entity and can only be differentiated verbally. At the time of meditative equipoise on emptiness, subject and object become one inseparable entity, and, since our ordinary expressions and conceptions cannot convey this state, it is called 'unthinkable' and 'inexpressible'. This is an undifferentiability of method and wisdom passed beyond all limits of the elaborations of thought, an undifferentiability of bliss and emptiness, an indivisibility of the two truths, a union. These are the best words of description and must be understood; without these most profound expressions any verbalisation is insufficient. Within the context of not distinguishing between the objective clear light and the subjective clear light, Nyingmapas emphasise this undifferentiability when they speak of the view. Thus, in terms of this view there is indeed a difference between the Perfection Vehicle and the Mantra Vehicle.

As the Gelukpa Jam-yang-shay-ba says, the objective clear light—emptiness, the principal object—is taught in sutra just as it is in tantra, but the subjective clear light—the extremely subtle fundamental innate mind of clear light—is taught only in Highest Yoga Tantra, not even in the three lower tantras and, of course, not in the Perfection Vehicle. Therefore, the view free of the elaborations of thought which is so frequently mentioned in the old translation school of Nyingma refers to the element of clear light without any differentiation of subject and object. This is called the essential purity, which is an affirming negative, not a non-affirming negative as emptiness is.

In the books of the new translation orders this clear light is called the completion stage of ultimate clear light and is even called the ultimate truth. For example, in the Perfection Vehicle, the Svatantrika-Madhyamikas present a metaphoric ultimate truth referring to a mind that has emptiness as its object. Similarly, when Highest Yoga Mantra presents the conventional stage of completion—illusory body—and an ultimate stage of completion—clear light—the word 'ultimate' does not refer to the object, emptiness, but to the subject cognising emptiness. The reason for this is that the mind has become undifferentiable from its object, emptiness, and thus is called an ultimate truth or a metaphoric ultimate truth. In this way the term 'ultimate truth' is also used frequently in the books of the new translation orders to refer to more than just emptiness.

Within this context there is a difference in view between Sutra and Mantra. Therefore, when Tsong-ka-pa says that with regard to the view of the middle way there is no presentation superior to that of Nagarjuna's *Treatise on the Middle Way*, he is referring to the objective clear light, emptiness. It is free of all dualistic elaborations, and, as the Sakya Pandita says, there can be no difference between Sutra and Mantra with respect to this.

The Perfection Vehicle and the Mantra Vehicle also cannot be differentiated through practice of the six perfections. In Mantra it is necessary to train in giving, ethics, patience, and so forth during six sessions daily, dividing the day into six portions. Failure to do this is considered an infraction. Therefore, the presence or the absence of practising the six perfections cannot differentiate the two vehicles.

The basic path for achieving a Buddha's Form Body is method—the altruistic mind of enlightenment induced by love and compassion. The basic path for achieving a

57

Buddha's Truth Body is the wisdom cognising emptiness. In Sutra and Mantra there is no difference with respect to these basic paths. Thus, from the viewpoint of the path that is practised, its basis—altruistic mind generation—and its deeds—the six perfections including the wisdom cognising emptiness—there is no difference. Also, small differences in path cannot be the differentiators of the Perfection and Mantra Vehicles.

The two vehicles cannot be differentiated by way of practitioners from the viewpoint of gradations in sharpness and dullness because if they were, the Perfection Vehicle itself would have to be divided into many vehicles. The swiftness or slowness of practitioners' progress on the path also cannot serve as the differentiator since many differences in speed are set forth in the Perfection Vehicle.

How, then, are the two vehicles differentiated? Some say that the difference between Sutra and Mantra is that Mantra was taught for those who can use desire as an aid in the path whereas the Perfection Vehicle was taught in order to tame beings within the context of separation from desire. This opinion is wrong because both the Perfection Vehicle and the Mantra Vehicle have modes of advancing on the path without having abandoned desire and both have modes of progress by cultivating paths to abandon desire. In Sutra it is said that just as the filth of a city is helpful to the field of a sugar-cane grower who knows how to utilise a substance which itself is not helpful, so the afflictions can be useful in the path. If one knows how to use the afflictions for the welfare of others, they can serve as aids in amassing the accumulations of merit, and in this sense desire is not one-pointedly to be avoided although, from the viewpoint of the entities of the afflictions, they are indeed to be abandoned.

Sutra Bodhisattvas who have not yet thoroughly abandoned the afflictions of desire and hatred can use them for the benefit of others, as in the cases of Bodhisattva kings who have fathered many children in order to further the welfare of the country through the work of their children. Here the afflictions act as secondary causes in the aiding of others.

Just as within Sutra practice there are occasions when Bodhisattvas intentionally do not abandon afflictions but use them as aids, so in Mantra practice, according to the time and the situation, Bodhisattvas use the afflictions. However, on occasions when there is no purpose for desire or hatred, a Mantra practitioner must intentionally seek to abandon them. If in order to be a practitioner of Mantra one necessarily had to have not abandoned desire and hatred, there would be no opportunity to become a Buddha through the Mantra path.

Others hold the more refined position that the division between Sutra and Tantra is determined by the special or main trainees initially engaging in those vehicles who either can or cannot use desire as an aid to the path. In general, it is true that using four types of joy arising from four types of desire—looking, laughing, embracing, and union—as favourable circumstances for cultivating the path occurs in the four sets of tantras. Thus, with regard to initial practitioners of the Perfection and Mantra Vehicles it can be said that the one is not able and the other is able to use such desire in the path. However, this cannot be posited as the differentiator between the paths of the two vehicles. Although it indicates an inequality in the capacities of the two types of persons, it is not the profound and complete distinction between the Perfection and Mantra Vehicles.

Others say that the bliss arising from concentration on the channels, winds, and drops [see note 68] differentiates the two vehicles, but this is a feature only of Highest Yoga Tantra, not of Mantra in general. Thus, it cannot serve as the distinction between the two vehicles.

Greatness of Mantra

The difference between the Perfection and Mantra Vehicles must apply to one of the two meanings of 'vehicle': the means by which one proceeds or the fruit to which one proceeds. There is no difference in the fruit, Buddhahood; hence, the difference rests in the sense of 'vehicle' as the means by which one progresses to that fruit.

Mahayana is superior to Hinayana in terms of method, the altruistic aspiration to highest enlightenment for the sake of all sentient beings, and the division of Mahayana into a Perfection Vehicle and a Mantra Vehicle is also made by way of method. In general, the paths included within the factor of method are the means for achieving a Buddha's Form Body whereas the paths included within the factor of wisdom are the means for achieving a Buddha's Truth Body. To achieve a Truth Body one needs to cultivate a path similar in aspect to a Truth Body, and both the Perfection and Mantra Vehicles have a path of wisdom in which one cultivates a similitude of a Buddha's Truth Body: the cognition of emptiness in space-like meditative equipoise.

In order to achieve a Form Body, one needs to cultivate a path that is similar in aspect to a Buddha's Form Body. Only Mantra has the special method for achieving this feat by cultivating paths that are similar in aspect to a Buddha's Form Body. The presence of meditation that utilises a similitude of a Form Body is the greatness of the Mantra method; such is not set forth in Sutra.

In order to remove mental defilements it is necessary to meditate on emptiness, but this is not a complete method for achieving Buddhahood because meditation on emptiness only removes the conception of inherent existence and all the afflictions that are based on it; other practices are needed in order to achieve the physical perfection of a Buddha. The complete method capable of bestowing Buddhahood quickly is the cultivation of a path of deity yoga in which the pride of being the deity of the effect state is established.

The attainment sought is the state of a Buddha endowed with the major and minor marks. To achieve this state one must train in the path of a divine body similar in aspect to the body of a Buddha. Therefore, cultivation of a divine body is not used merely for the achievement of common feats but is essential for achieving the uncommon feat of a Buddha's Form Body.

According to the Perfection Vehicle, in order for the wisdom cognising emptiness to serve as an antidote to the obstructions to omniscience, it must be conjoined with altruistic mind generation and practice of the perfections. The vast methods such as giving, ethics, and patience help limitless sentient beings, and their imprint at Buddhahood is the achievement of Form Bodies which perform limitless altruistic activities.

The wisdom penetrating the depth of the suchness of phenomena is the means for actualising the non-conceptual wisdom consciousness of a Buddha. Thus, the special imprint of the collection of wisdom is the attainment of the Wisdom Truth Body coupled with the abandonment of all contaminations.

Neither a Truth Body nor a Form Body is attained singly because they both depend on completion of these causal collections of method and wisdom. The two collections act as co-operating cause and special cause of the Truth and Form Bodies. For example, an eye consciousness is generated in dependence on three causes, an object, an eye sense, and a former moment of consciousness; the ability of an eye consciousness to apprehend colour and shape rather than sound is the imprint of the eye sense; its being a conscious entity is the imprint of an immediately preceding moment of consciousness; and its being generated in the image of a particular object is the imprint of the object. Just as each of the three causes is said to have its own individual imprint in the generation of the eye consciousness, the imprint of wisdom is a Truth Body and the imprint of method is a Form Body.

Because the Perfection Vehicle sets forth a method for achieving the non-conceptual Wisdom Body of a Buddha and the Form Bodies effecting limitless maturations of other beings' minds, it is *said* to have unsurpassed method. However, in the path of the Perfection Vehicle, the causes of highest enlightenment are explained as only the six perfections. These are not sufficient because through cultivating causes such as giving, ethics, patience, and so forth—that are different in aspect from Form Bodies, the fruit—one cannot actualise the enlightenment of a Buddha. One would be attempting to actualise an effect that is different in aspect from the causes. The effect of Buddhahood, which has a nature of profundity—a Truth Body—and vastness—a Form Body adorned with the major and minor marks—in one undifferentiable entity, is achieved from causes that have a similar nature. Just as one meditates on the meaning of selflessness that is similar in aspect to a Truth Body, so one should cultivate paths of vastness that are similar in aspect to a Form Body.

In the Mantra Vehicle the 'vast' refers to the appearance of a divine body. There is a vastness at the time of the path—cultivation of the vivid appearance of a divine body coupled with divine pride—and a vastness at the time of the fruit—an ultimate vastness that achieves the welfare of others. Deity yoga is 'vast' because deities such as Vairochana, who are qualified by emptiness and included within the factor of appearance, are inexhaustible, continual, limitless, and pure. Even though both pure and impure phenomena are qualified by emptiness, there is said to be a difference due to the phenomena qualified by it.

In Mantra, conjunction of method with wisdom and vice versa means not that method and wisdom are individual entities which are merely compatible with each other but that they are complete within the entity of one mind. Based on cultivating this union of method and wisdom, at Buddhahood the Truth Body of non-dual wisdom itself appears as the features of a deity. Therefore, prior to meditating on a divine body it is necessary to establish through reasoning the non-inherent existence of oneself. Then, within the context of meditating on this emptiness, just that mind which has one's own emptiness as its object serves as the basis of appearance of the deity.

Induced by ascertaining the emptiness of one's own inherent existence, this consciousness itself appears in the form of the face, arms, and so forth of a deity. The wisdom consciousness vividly appears as a divine body and at the same time ascertains its non-inherent existence. These two—the wisdom cognising non-inherent existence and the mind of deity yoga—are one entity, but posited to be different from the viewpoint of their imprints. Thus, from a conventional point of view method and wisdom are different within the context of being one entity. They are said to be different in that method is the exclusion of non-method and wisdom is the exclusion of non-wisdom.

Based on the appearance of a divine body, the pride of being that deity develops, having ultimate and conventional aspects. Some scholars say that the appearance of a mind ascertaining emptiness in the form of a deity means that this one mind has emptiness as its referent object and a divine body as its appearing object. Thus, the consciousness has a factor of ascertain-ment—the understanding of a negative of inherent existence—and a factor of appearance—the vivid reflection of a divine body. In this way, divine pride has two aspects, observing the ultimate—emptiness—and observing the conventional—a divine body.

Among the sutra interpretations there are two systems with regard to whether a phenomenon qualified by emptiness appears to a mind that inferentially cognises that emptiness. Some say that an object qualified by an empty nature appears during inferential cognition of its emptiness, and others say that the appearance of the object is no longer present when its emptiness is being understood. In Tsong-ka-pa's *Great Exposition of the Stages of the Path Common to the Vehicles*, it seems that the phenomenon qualified by emptiness does appear to an inferential consciousness cognising emptiness, but in some monastery textbooks the opposite is held. In any case, initially one meditates on an emptiness, and then, within the context of the mind's continuous ascertainment of emptiness, the meditator believes that he is using this mind as the basis [or source] of appearance. At that time, the sense of a mere 'I' designated in dependence on the pure resident—the deity—and residence—the palace and surroundings—is a fully qualified divine pride. As much as one can cultivate such pride, so much does one harm the conception of inherent existence that is the root of cyclic existence.

This composite of method and wisdom—the appearance of a deity empty of true existence, like an illusion—is an affirming negative, an absence of inherent existence as well as a positive appearance. One gradually becomes accustomed to this mind, and finally when one arrives at high levels on the stage of completion as explained in Highest Yoga Tantra, the union of a learner is attained in which a continual similitude of a Form Body and a Truth Body is actualised. These are a 'Form Body' on the occasion of the path and a wisdom mind of clear light, which are the actual substantial causes of Buddhahood.

Thus, Mantra is distinguished from the Perfection Vehicle through its superior method for the achievement of a Form Body. Mere meditation on a divine body that is not related with meditation on emptiness is not sufficient because the branch of wisdom is not complete. On the other hand, mere meditation on emptiness is also not sufficient. Even though it is not possible to attain Buddhahood in dependence on the paths of the Perfection Vehicle alone, the Perfection Vehicle does set forth paths for the achievement of Buddhahood. If one engages in these paths, meditating on emptiness and cultivating the features of method as explained in the Perfection Vehicle, then it is said that one will attain Buddhahood only after many countless aeons; one cannot attain Buddhahood quickly. Actually, one cannot attain Buddhahood through causes that do not have an aspect similar to the effect, a Form Body. In brief, the Body of a Buddha is attained through meditating on it. One should meditate on a divine body until its features appear clearly and steadily, until it seems that one can touch it with one's hand and can see it with one's eye.

Someone might think that in the Perfection Vehicle one cultivates a Buddha's Form Body through meditation involving prayer petitions to attain such. However, if that were the case, one would not need to meditate on emptiness in order to attain a Truth Body; planting prayer petitions would be sufficient. Buddhahood is attained through the non-dual yoga of the profound and the manifest; without it Buddhahood is impossible.

This is established not only in Highest Yoga Tantra but also in the other three tantras. In Action and Performance Tantra a Truth Body, which is said to be thoroughly pure in the sense of being free of all dualistic elaborations, is achieved through the yoga of signlessness—meditation on emptiness—and a Form Body, which is said to be 'impure' in the sense that it is involved in duality, is achieved through the yoga with signs—deity yoga. In Yoga Tantra deity yoga is presented in conjunction with five factors, called the five clarifications.

This yoga of the union of the profound and manifest is the path of all the *chief* trainees of the Vajra Vehicle but not necessarily of *all* trainees of the Vajra Vehicle. For those who cannot imagine themselves as deities, the practice of contemplation of a deity in front of oneself is set forth in conjunction with repeating mantra, making petitions, and so forth. The chief trainees in terms of whom the Vajra Vehicle was taught are those capable of practising the full Mantra path, and generating oneself as a deity is definitely taught for all chief trainees. The modes of meditation for the achievement of feats, such as the techniques for meditating on the winds (*prāṇa*), are all for the sake of either making deity yoga more firm or enhancing cognition of suchness.

Clarification

Mantra uses the effect as the path in the sense that a path similar in aspect to the effect is cultivated. In both the Perfection and Mantra Vehicles one cultivates a path similar in aspect to a Truth Body, but in the Mantra Vehicle one also cultivates a path similar in aspect to a Form Body. In this way, the Mantra Vehicle is superior to the Perfection Vehicle.

Wrong idea: Deity yoga is unnecessary

Someone might object: 'To achieve a body adorned with the auspicious marks of a Universal Monarch, it is not necessary to cultivate a path of meditation that is similar in aspect to the body of a Universal Monarch [see note 62]. Thus, it is not established that in order to achieve an effect one must cultivate a cause that accords in aspect with that effect. What is the reason for singling out Buddhahood as requiring a cause similar in aspect to the effect?'

Answer: According to the Perfection Vehicle, in general a Form Body is achieved through the amassing of merit. In particular, when a Bodhisattva arrives on the eighth among the ten grounds, he newly achieves a mental body that has similitudes of a Buddha's major and minor marks and arises in dependence on the stage of latent predispositions of ignorance [the motivation of wishing to assume a mental body] and non-contaminated action [the mental factor of intention which is the subtle exertion involved in the motivation of wishing to assume a mental body]. This body gradually improves and eventually turns into the Form Body of a Buddha. Thus, even the Perfection Vehicle does not say that merely amassing the

67

collections of merit is sufficient, or that at Buddhahood one newly achieves a Form Body the continuum of which did not exist before. In the systems of both Sutra and Tantra it is necessary to achieve a similitude of a Form Body prior to attaining Buddhahood.

According to Highest Yoga Tantra, some persons attain Buddhahood in one lifetime, and because these persons are not born with a body adorned with the major and minor marks they must achieve such a body through the practice of deity yoga. These are not cases of taking birth as a Form Body and thus are not similar to the accumulation of causes that impel one into a rebirth as a universal monarch or as an animal, hungry ghost, or hell-being. In the case of rebirth it is not necessary to accumulate causes that are similar in *aspect* to the particular type of rebirth being impelled. There is a great difference between a cause projecting rebirth and a cause of similar type.

Meditation on oneself as undifferentiable from a deity is the special cause of similar type for attaining Buddhahood. If one meditated only on emptiness and did not cultivate any method—either that of the Perfection or that of the Mantra Vehicle—one would fall to the fruit of a Hinayana Foe Destroyer. In order to attain the definite goodness of the highest achievement, Buddhahood, deity yoga is needed. Also, in order to attain the common achievements, the eight feats and so forth, one must view one's body clearly as a divine body and train in the pride of being a deity. Without deity yoga the Mantra path is impossible; deity yoga is the essence of Mantra.

Meditating on oneself as having a divine body seems to be childish play, like telling a story to a child to stimulate his imagination. However, in conjunction with the view of emptiness, altruistic motivation, and knowledge of its purpose, it is a very important psychological train-ing—viewing one's body in the form of a deity, generating the pride of being a deity, temporarily performing the activities of pacification and so forth, and ultimately achieving Buddhahood. There is a difference in force between merely repeating a mantra and repeating that mantra within the context of deity yoga; there may in time be a scientific explanation of this difference.

Wrong idea: The Buddhahood of the Perfection Vehicle and the Buddhahood of the Vajra Vehicle are different

Although there is a difference between the Perfection and Mantra Vehicles in terms of method and many forms of paths, there is no difference in the fruit, the Buddhahood that is sought by both. In some scriptures Buddhahood and Vajradharahood seem to be different, and thus some have thought that the fruits of the two vehicles must be different and that Vajradharahood is higher than Buddhahood. This confusion sometimes arises because a tenth ground Bodhisattva is often referred to as a 'Buddha' although he is not yet an actual Buddha.

Although practice of only the Perfection Vehicle is not sufficient to achieve Buddhahood, the Buddhahood described in the Perfection and Mantra Vehicles is the same. It is incorrect to say that Buddhahood can be achieved solely through the paths of the Perfection Vehicle and that upon attaining Buddhahood one must enter into the Mantra Vehicle to achieve an even higher fruit. Even though one must finally engage in Mantra in order to become a Buddha, it can be said in general that the Perfection and Mantra paths achieve the same fruit, with their difference lying in the speed with which the fruit is attained.

It cannot be said that *in general* Buddhahood can be achieved through Mantra in the one lifetime of this degenerate age without depending on practice over countless aeons because this cannot be done following the paths of the lower tantras alone. One must finally enter

69

Highest Yoga Tantra in order to achieve Buddhahood without practising for countless aeons. According to Tsong-ka-pa's *Great Exposition of Secret Mantra* the attainment of Buddhahood in one lifetime is a distinguishing feature of Highest Yoga Tantra.

The paths of the three lower tantras are faster than the Perfection path in that the paths of accumulation and preparation do not require one countless aeon of practice, but their mode of procedure on the paths of seeing and meditation is similar to that of the Perfection Vehicle. However, it must be taken into account that Action, Performance, and Yoga Tantras say that Buddhahood can be achieved in one lifetime. For instance, the continuation of the *Vairochanabhisambodhi Tantra (Vairochanābhisaṃbodhi),* a Performance Tantra, says, 'Those Bodhisattvas engaging in practice from the approach of Secret Mantra will become completely and perfectly enlightened in just this lifetime.' Such statements that enlightenment can be achieved in one lifetime by means of the three lower tantras should be taken as an exaggerated expression of the greatness of that particular tantra.

Practitioners of the three lower tantras attain many common feats through which they see Buddhas and Bodhisattvas, hear their teachings, and under their care complete the practices for enlightenment quickly, but aside from proceeding faster on the paths of accumulation and preparation, the rest of the path is still protracted. According to the oral tradition, attainment of Buddhahood in the one short lifetime *of this degenerate era* [which nowadays is roughly sixty years] is a distinguishing feature of Highest Yoga Tantra, but the attainment of the enlightenment of Buddhahood in one lifetime is also a feature of the three lower tantras. The latter is not the one short lifetime of the degenerate era but refers to the ability gained by yogis through the practice of deity yoga, repetition of mantra, and so forth to extend their lifetime over many aeons. During such a lifetime one can attain highest enlightenment, relying on the paths of the three lower tantras and eventually engaging in Highest Yoga. The passage in the *Vairochanabhisambodhi Tantra* may refer to such a long lifetime.

Wrong idea: The stage of generation is just deity yoga

Shantideva says in his *Engaging in the Bodhisattva Deeds* that when a Bodhisattva who has attained a ground gives away his own body he has no physical suffering and thus no mental suffering and thereby can easily give away even his body if needed. Also, the *Meeting of Father and Son Sutra (Pitāputrasamāgama)* says that Bodhisattvas can maintain a blissful feeling in all situations, even during torture. Based on such teachings, Ratnarakshita mistakenly propounds that the great bliss generated in the Perfection Vehicle is the same as that generated in Highest Yoga Tantra. However, he correctly asserts that both the Mantra and Perfection Vehicles involve meditation on emptiness and also correctly points out that in the Perfection Vehicle Bodhisattvas on certain occasions use the desire realm attributes of pleasant forms, sounds, odours, tastes and tangible objects and that, therefore, the usage of desire in the path is not a distinguishing feature of the Mantra Vehicle. He cites the *Kashyapa Chapter Sutra (Kāshyapaparivarta)*:

> Just as the filth of city-dwellers
> Helps the field of a sugar-cane grower,
> So the manure of a Bodhisattva's afflictions
> Assists in growing the qualities of a Buddha.

He also correctly notes that an altruistic aspiration to highest enlightenment, induced by love and compassion, is common to both the Perfection and Mantra Vehicles. However, he mistakenly concludes that the distinctive feature of tantra is the stage of generation. He wrongly assumes that the stage of generation in Highest Yoga Tantra is primarily deity yoga and that the stage of completion is primarily meditation on emptiness, whereas the very foundation of deity yoga is meditation on emptiness and deity yoga also occurs in the stage of completion.

Wrong idea: Usage of desire in the path is for low trainees

Tripitakamala says that even though the aim of the two vehicles—Buddhahood—is the same, the Mantra Vehicle surpasses the Perfection Vehicle by way of four features:

> The first feature is that practitioners of Mantra are not obscured whereas those of the Perfection Vehicle are. Practitioners of Mantra realise that the completion of a perfection is a fruit of meditative stabilisation and that one cannot complete a perfection through actually giving away one's own body and so forth. Practitioners of the Perfection Vehicle do not realise this and thus are obscured.

This interpretation is wrong because in the Perfection Vehicle itself Shantideva says that since we see that there are still beggars in the world and since we know that the earlier Buddhas and Bodhisattvas achieved a perfection of giving, the perfection of giving could not involve eliminating all poverty in the world. Rather, the perfection of giving is the full development of an attitude of generosity—the completion of the thought to give away all of one's possessions, along with all effects that might arise from them, to all sentient beings. According to Shantideva, a perfection depends on the mind. Therefore,

Tripitakamala's explanation of the feature of non-obscuration is not feasible.

The second feature is that the Mantra Vehicle has many methods whereas the Perfection Vehicle does not. In the Perfection Vehicle one proceeds only by peaceful means, but the Mantra Vehicle has four divisions which each have many techniques to counter one problem. For instance, for the desirous and the proud Mantra has many methods such as imagining oneself as any of a great number of deities.

Tripitakamala's explanation of this feature appears to be correct, but it cannot serve as a reason for dividing Mahayana into a Perfection Vehicle and a Mantra Vehicle because Highest Yoga Tantra, for instance, has many techniques which the other three tantras do not have, but it is not a separate vehicle.

The third feature is that the Perfection Vehicle involves asceticism whereas the Mantra Vehicle does not. Jnanakirti and Tripitakamala explain that Mantra has two types of trainees: those without desire for a Knowledge Woman [see note 72] and those with desire. Those without desire for a Knowledge Woman are the highest trainees, and they meditate on the actual great seal which is a union of method and wisdom. Those with desire are divided into two groups: those without desire for an external Knowledge Woman and those with desire for an external Knowledge Woman. The former meditate on an imagined Knowledge Woman, and the latter use an actual Knowledge Woman.

This interpretation is wrong because among the trainees of Highest Yoga Tantra those having the sharpest faculties use desire for an external Knowledge Woman in the path. It is through this means that 'jewel-like persons' achieve

Buddhahood in one lifetime. Since both vehicles have cultivation of paths free of desire and paths using desire, this feature cannot distinguish the two vehicles.

Tripitakamala's explanation of the fourth feature, sharpness of faculties, is also incorrect because if he means non-obscuration with respect to method his explanation of the difference in method has already been shown to be inadequate. If he means that in Mantra desire for the attributes of the desire realm is used in the path, then he is also wrong because according to his faulty explanation the best of sharp trainees do not have such, whereas they actually do.

Wrong idea: The four sets of tantras correspond to the four castes

There are four sets of tantras: Action, Performance, Yoga, and Highest Yoga. Some also divide Highest Yoga into father tantra, mother tantra, and non-dual tantra, making six. According to Tsong-ka-pa, 'non-dual tantra' refers to a non-duality of method and wisdom—great bliss and emptiness; therefore, he says that all Highest Yoga Tantras are non-dual tantras. The translator Tak-tsang (sTag-tshang), however, asserts that the *Kalachakra Tantra* is a non-dual tantra because it emphasises the fourth initiation which is concerned with a union of supreme immutable bliss and totally supreme emptiness. For him dualistic tantras emphasise either one of these two.

Practitioners of the four tantras have the same intention in that they all are seeking others' welfare. The object of attainment—the Buddhahood which is the extinguishment of all faults and fulfilment of all auspicious attributes—is the same for all. Therefore, the four tantras cannot be divided from the viewpoint of field of intent or object of attainment. All four have deity yoga, and variations of

74

deity yoga are not sufficient to serve as the difference between them because each of the four also has many forms of deity yoga. Although there are sources in Indian texts that say that the four tantras are for the four castes or those dominated by particular afflictions, these cannot serve as the differentiators of the four tantras or even indicate a predominance among their trainees.

The tantras were mainly expounded for those of the desire realm and specifically for those seeking enlightenment by way of using desire in the path. The sets of tantras are differentiated by way of four modes of practice and four types of trainees whose abilities correspond to these four types of practice. These are four ways of using desire in the path based on differing capacities for generating the emptiness and deity yogas.

Among the seven branches—complete enjoyment, union, great bliss, non-inherent existence, compassion, uninterrupted continuity, and non-cessation—three are found only in tantra—complete enjoyment, union, and great bliss—and the other four are common to both sutra and tantra although non-inherent existence can also be put in the group specific to tantra when it is considered as the object ascertained by a bliss consciousness. The three lower tantras do not set forth the branch of union; also, in the lower tantras one does not take cognisance of an external Knowledge Woman and then use desire in the path, but takes cognisance only of a meditated Knowledge Woman. In Yoga Tantras the bliss arising from holding hands or embracing is used in the path; in Performance Tantras, from laughing; and in Action Tantras, from looking. In brief, the four tantras are similar in that they all use desire for the attributes of the desire realm on the path.

In Action Tantras external activities predominate. In Performance Tantras external activities and internal yoga are performed equally. In Yoga Tantras internal yoga is predominant. In Highest Yoga Tantras a path unequalled by any other is taught. These etymological descriptions of the names of the four tantras apply to their main trainees but not to all their trainees, because, for instance, it is said that even some Yoga Tantras were set forth for those frightened by meditation on oneself as a deity.

The four tantras are distinguished by way of their main trainees' abilities and not by way of those who merely have an interest in them, because, as is the case nowadays, there are many who take an interest in a path for which they have no capacity.

Initiation

A mandala is said to be extremely profound because meditation on it serves as an antidote, quickly eradicating the obstructions to liberation and the obstructions to omniscience as well as their latent predispositions. It is difficult for those of low intellect to penetrate its significance.

There is a difference between entering a mandala and receiving initiation. In order merely to enter a mandala it is sufficient to have faith; it is not necessary to have generated the altruistic mind of enlightenment. Also, one may enter a mandala and receive initiation without having fully generated the altruistic mind of enlightenment, but it is necessary for one who is training in the two stages of Highest Yoga Tantra to have done so.

In the past, entrance into a mandala and granting initiation were used very carefully, discriminating between the two, but nowadays Tibetans tend to initiate anyone. Vajradhara set forth a complete system with different levels—those who could just enter a mandala, those who could also receive the water and head-dress initiations, and so forth. When it is done systematically, the lama, prior to granting initiation, analyses the student to determine whether he or she can engage in the three trainings [ethics, meditative stabilisation and wisdom] and keep the vows. He allows those who are not qualified but who have great faith to enter a mandala but does not allow initiation. These systematic restrictions, which when followed make initiation effective and practical, are often not followed nowadays, causing trouble for both lama and initiate.

There is a story about Druk-pa kun-lek who was visiting

an area where a lama was bestowing initiation. When the lama passed by, all thereabouts rose and paid him respect, but Druk-pa-kun-lek did not. The lama playfully asked him what he was doing. 'When I pass by, other people pay respect. Why are you displaying this ill behaviour?' Druk-pa-kun-lek answered by asking, 'Are you giving many initiations? Are you causing many to fall from their vows and pledges? Are you opening the way to hell for many?'

If you are able to think about the meaning of cyclic existence in general and human life in particular, then it is possible to discipline the mind through religious practice which is the process of becoming peaceful and anxiety-free. Otherwise, if too much emphasis is put on the sufferings of the hells and the imminence of death, there is a chance of falling into paralysing fear. There is a story in Tibet about an abbot of a monastery who went to give a discourse. A fellow asked the abbot's servant where the abbot had gone, and the servant said, 'He has gone to frighten old men and women.' If you fulfil the value of a human lifetime through engaging in religious practice, then there is no point in worrying about death.

Initially, you should take refuge in the Three Jewels from the round orb of your heart, then take a vow of individual emancipation, and after that generate the aspirational and practical minds of enlightenment. Then, when you arrive at the point where it is suitable to hear tantra, you should receive teachings on Ashvaghosha's *Twenty Stanzas on the Bodhisattva Vow (Bodhisattva-saṃvaravimshaka)* and *Fifty Stanzas on the Guru (Guru-pañchāshikā)*. Then you may receive initiation.

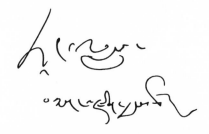

The Buddhist monk, Tenzin Gyatso
BE 2518, AD 1974, the Tibetan year
of the Fire Tiger.

II
The Great Exposition of Secret Mantra

The Stages of the Path to a Conqueror and Pervasive
Master, a Great Vajradhara: Revealing All Secret Topics

TSONG-KA-PA

Part One

Translated and edited by Jeffrey Hopkins
Associate editors: Lati Rinpochay and Geshe Gedün Lodrö

Reasons for Faith

I bow down and go for refuge with great respect in all my births to the lotus feet of the excellent gurus and the venerable Manjughosha [Manjushri].

Homage to the Spiritual Guides

Homage to the feet of the excellent guides,
Who through their mind of mercy teach as it is,
By one's respectfully taking their lotus feet to
   the top of one's head,
The stainless path removing the faults of
   cyclic existence and mere peace.

Homage to Vajradhara

May I be protected by the lord of mandalas,
Who like a captivating rainbow in the
   stainless sky
Stirs not from the state of complete
   extinction of all conceptual elaborations
And emanates countless hosts of deities
   through the physical creations of his sport.

Homage to Vajrapani

Through my bowing with great respect to the
   powerful protector,
The master bearing the knowledge mantras, the
   collector of all
The secret topics spoken by him,[1]
The hosts of demons should now take heed.

Homage to Manjughosha

O Manjughosha, sole father of all the
    Conquerors,
You are a treasure of wisdom such that
    having heard
That you bestow the superior gift of
    discrimination with a glance
Of pleasure, granting realisation of the
    profound thought of the Conquerors,
I have relied on you continually for a long
    time
As my special god and will not forsake your
    lotus feet.
For me there is never another refuge.
O Manjughosha, grant the fruit of my wishes.

Reasons for Composing the Book

I have been beseeched by many wishing to
    practise
The tantras correctly as they are taught by
    the wise
And by one speaking the two languages
With extensive knowledge of countless books.[2]

I have been strongly beseeched again and
    again by one
Sparkling with many merits at the forefront
    of all beings,
A good being of unusual thought bearing the
    burden of spreading
The glorious Vajra Vehicle in all directions.[3]

Those satisfied with but a part who
    treat not the great systems as precepts,

Those who cannot analyse with faultless reason
  what the scriptures mean,
Those who are learned but make no effort
To achieve cannot please the Conquerors.

Promise to Compose the Book

Having seen thus and with my mind profoundly
Affected by the deeds of the excellent
Of the past who practised well the teaching
I will strive to clarify their system.

For this effort may the hosts of Sky Goers—
Field-born, innate and mantra-born—regard me
With love like a mother for her son, granting
  all the feats
And bestowing the kindness of removing all
  obstacles.

There are those whose capacity of the Mahayana lineage is not meagre, whose minds are strongly moved by great compassion through having trained in the common path sustained by a spiritual guide, an excellent protector. They are in great haste to free from cyclic existence the kind mothers wandering there. They should enter the short path, the profound Vajra Vehicle that quickly bestows the state of a Blessed Buddha, the sole refuge of all sentient beings. Therefore, I will explain here the stages of the path to [the state of] a great Vajradhara.

The explanation has two parts: showing that only the Conqueror's teaching is the entrance for those wishing liberation, and describing the doors of the different stages for entry to the teaching.

Only the Conqueror's Teaching is the Entrance for
Those Wishing Liberation

Once one begins analysing the great aims of oneself and others, there is no satisfaction with merely the system revealed by the elders of the world—the achievement of happiness and avoidance of suffering as long as one lives. The entrance for those seeking the higher features of future lives and above [liberation from cyclic existence and the attainment of omniscience] is only the teaching of the Blessed Buddha whose banner flies over the three realms. He is the great base of the welfare of all beings; the mere movement of his breath in and out is a great means providing medicine for sentient beings. For he attained his supreme glorious state through having practised the aspiration to highest enlightenment for the sake of all sentient beings and through the great waves of the deeds of Buddha Sons that are induced by this altruistic mind of enlightenment. The mind of enlightenment is a cherishing of others more than oneself—a source of talk that accords not at all with the world since most other persons find it difficult even to take delight in it from the depths of their heart.

Matrcheta [Ashvaghosha] and Dignaga's *Interwoven Praise (Mishrakastotra)*[a] says:

> I dwell in an ocean of cyclic
> Existence of depth without limit.
> The frightful sea monsters of desire
> And so forth are eating my body.
> Where will I go for refuge now?
>
> If one has intelligence,
> One would take refuge in him,
> The one who has
> Not any defects
> Who in every way has all
> Auspicious attributes.
> It would be right to praise and respect
> Him and to abide in his teaching.

Nevertheless, Kapila and the others—even though they did not know the path of liberation—were maddened by the poison of pride and claimed to be teachers. Wishing to teach a suchness of phenomena in a way other than that taught by the Sugatas,[5] they wrote many books that were made to appear like a correct path and advised those wishing liberation. However, only the completely perfect Buddha, his teaching, and those properly learning it are the teacher, the path, and friends on the journey to liberation for those wishing liberation. Teachers, teachings, and their students other that these are not.

You must gain unmoving conviction in the source of refuge. Thereby you will realise that only the Subduer's teaching is the entrance for those wishing liberation. Those with little force of mind will determine this merely through an assumption, but those with strong minds should seek firm conviction induced by valid cognition. Otherwise it will only be an assertion.

Further, Shamkarapati's *Praise of the Supra-Divine (Devātishayastotra)*[6] says:

> I am not a partisan of Buddha,
> I do not hate Kapila and the others,
> I hold as a teacher only
> Him whose word possesses reason.

You should forsake partisanship and hatred for the systems of your own and others' teachers and analyse which of them provide good or bad explanations. Then, you should adopt only that which shows the means of attaining the two aims of trainees [high status within cyclic existence and the definite goodness of liberation and omniscience] and provides correct proofs. The scriptures of the two systems are what are to be analysed to find which does or does not bear the truth; thus, it would not be suitable to cite them as a proof [of their own truth]. Only reasoning distinguishes what is or is not true.

The manner of reasoning is this: It is indeed true that in terms of the order in which they are generated in a person's continuum one first achieves the temporary attainment of high status and later definite goodness. However, when scriptures showing the two aims of beings are analysed to find whether they are false or not, one first establishes through reasoning that a system is not deceptive about the principal aim of definite goodness. Then one can infer from this that the system is not deceptive with respect to the secondary attainment of high status. This is the assertion of the scholar-kings. Dharmakirti's *Commentary on (Dignaga's) 'Compendium of Valid Cognition' (Pramāṇavarttika)*[7] says:

> Because the main meaning cannot be controverted,
> [The same] can be inferred with regard to the others.

Aryadeva's *Four Hundred (Chatuḥshataka)*[8] says:

> Whoever has generated doubt
> In Buddha's word on the non-manifest
> Will believe that only Buddha [is omniscient]
> Based on [his teaching about] emptiness.

One must logically establish both the existence of cyclic existence—the continuation of the aggregates of suffering through the source of conceiving self [inherent existence]—and the existence of the stages going to liberation—achievement of the state of freedom through the wisdom cognising selflessness. These should be proved with reasoning as they are in the logical systems.

If one said, 'Since these are extremely obscure for a common being, the only proof is scripture, and I go for refuge to you, O Blessed One, having abandoned other teachers,' one would be proclaiming the faults of one's own refuge. It would be like saying: 'Refuge is only one's own wish; there are no correct proofs.' For citation of scripture is not suitable as a proof, and you would be asserting that there are no logical proofs.

Furthermore, scriptures taught by our own and others' teachers disagree about whether or not there is rebirth, whether the mental and physical aggregates are permanent or impermanent, whether or not self exists, and so forth. When our own great schools and those of others debate the correctness or otherwise of these, we are not able to prove that the scriptures of our own teacher are correct [without relying on reasoning].

There are scriptures teaching very hidden topics that cannot be proved by the valid cognition of inference from evidence; they are proved to be unmistaken with respect to their contents by reasoning purified through the three analyses.[9] The establishment of the modes of the process is done through reasoning; one does not rely on asserting scripture as proof. Here I have only touched on the subject which I will explain in detail in other books.[10]

The scriptures of other schools that teach the chief aims of persons are only contradictory. For example, they propound that a permanent factor, such as a generality *(pradhāna)* or Lord· *(Īshvara)*, is the creator of cyclic existence, and they assert that those seeking liberation overcome that existence by cultivating the path. These are contradictory because without overcoming its main cause, cyclic existence cannot be overcome, while the cause could never be overcome if it were permanent. Similarly, it is contradictory to reject the view of selflessness and to take as an object of attainment a liberation that cuts the bonds to cyclic existence.

As explained above, the Three Refuges—our Teacher and so forth—are for those wishing liberation, and teachers and so forth who do not accord with them are never [final] refuges. If you have not induced conviction in this, you cannot have a firm mind, single-pointed with respect to your own source of refuge. The arising of such a firm mind relies on seeing, through reasoning, the faults and advantages of the two systems.

Therefore, whether or not a [non-Buddhist] Forder (*Tīrthika*) is actually present [to refute in debate] is inconsequential; if the intelligent wish to generate the special mind of refuge, they must do as was explained above [ascertaining through reasoning that the Three Jewels are the only refuges]. Thus, it should be known that the treatises of logic such as Dharmakirti's *Seven Treatises*[11] are a superior means of generating great respect, not merely verbal, for our own teacher Buddha, for his teaching—both verbal doctrine and that of realisation—and for proper practice.

Paths to Buddhahood

Doors of the Different Stages for Entry to the Teaching

This section has two parts: divisions of the vehicles in general and of Mahayana.

Divisions of the Vehicles in General

This section has four parts: how the vehicles are divided, reasons for and nature of the individual divisions, and a teaching that all of them are ultimately branches of the process of fullest enlightenment.

How the Vehicles are Divided

In Aryadeva's *Lamp Compendium of Practice (Charyāmelāpakapradīpa),*[12] the vehicles are divided through arranging practices into three types from the viewpoint of the three types of trainees' interests. Practices free from desire are taught to those interested in the lowly; practices of the grounds and perfections to those interested in the vast; and practices of desire to those specially interested in the profound. Similarly, Tripitakamala's *Lamp for the Three Modes (Nayatrayapradīpa)*[13] says:

> The meaning of the mode of
> The truths, of the perfections
> And of the great secret mantra
> Through abridgement has here been taught.

Thus, the master Tripitakamala includes all within three modes—that of the yoga of the four truths and so forth.

91

Jnanakirti also does the same in his *Abridged Explanation of All the Word (Tattvāvatārākhyasakalasugatavachastātparyavyākhyāprakaraṇa)*.[14]

Maitreya's *Ornament for the Mahayana Sutras (Mahāyānasūtrālaṃkāra)* says, 'The scriptural divisions are either two or three'. Thus, there are said to be two scriptural divisions, Mahayana and Hinayana [or three, discipline, sets of discourses, and knowledge]. It is permissible to use these explanations with reference both to divisions of scriptures and divisions of paths or vehicles.

Reasons for the Division

Let us explain the reasons for saying there are two divisions of scriptures and vehicles. There are low trainees who seek a low object of intention which is a low attainment solely for their own sake—the state of merely extinguishing the suffering of cyclic existence. There are supreme trainees who seek an elevated object of intention, the supreme attainment—the state of Buddhahood—for the sake of all sentient beings. Since there are these two types of trainees, low and high, the vehicles by which they go to their own state are called the Low Vehicle (*Hīnayāna*) and the Great Vehicle (*Mahāyāna*). Doctrines taught in accordance with these are called the scriptural divisions of Hinayana and Mahayana.

Hinayana has two types of followers, Hearers and Solitary Realisers, and the paths that lead them to their respective states are divided into a Hearer and a Solitary Realiser Vehicle. Thus, there are three vehicles [the Hearer, Solitary Realiser, and Mahayana ones].

Nature of the Individual Divisions

This section has two parts, presentation of Hinayana and of Mahayana.

Presentation of Hinayana

It is said in Asanga's *Actuality of the Levels (Bhūmivastu, Yogacharyābhūmi)* that though the faculties and fruits of Hearers and Solitary Realisers differ in their inferiority and superiority [the former being inferior to the latter], the presentations of their paths are mostly the same. Because I fear that the fine details would run to too many words, I will just summarise the coarse features common to both Hearers and Solitary Realisers.

Those who have Hearer and Solitary Realiser lineages have turned their backs on bearing the burden of others' welfare and are engaged only in their own liberation. The chief cause of attaining liberation is the wisdom cognising the meaning of selflessness because the chief cause of being bound in cyclic existence is the conception of self [inherent existence]; therefore, [not just Bodhisattvas but] also Hearers and Solitary Realisers, understanding this fact, seek this wisdom. They accompany it with other paths such as ethics and meditative stabilisation, and through having cultivated that wisdom they extinguish all afflictions.

Sautrantikas, Kashmiri Vaibhashikas, Chittamatrins and [Svatantrika] Madhyamikas [wrongly] hold that Hearers and Solitary Realisers do not realise that a person, even though empty of inherent existence in the sense of lacking natural existence, appears like a magician's illusion to exist inherently. They [wrongly] say that a cognition of a selflessness of persons involves realisation that persons do not have a substantially existent entity such as is imputed by non-Buddhists. The glorious Chandrakirti says that if that were so then Hearers and Solitary Realisers would never overcome the conception of true existence with respect to persons, and, therefore, such is not the meaning of cognising the selflessness of persons. For, as long as persons are conceived to exist truly, the conception of a self of persons has not been overcome.

93

Also, just as a cognition of a mental or physical aggregate or the like as not inherently existing must be put as the meaning of cognising the selflessness of phenomena [other than persons], so a cognition of a person as not inherently existing must mean the cognisance of the selflessness of persons. As long as the aggregates are conceived to exist truly, the conception that persons truly exist also operates. As long as this is so, one cannot overcome all afflictions. One would have to assert that, no matter how much effort were made by Hearers and Solitary Realisers, they could not be liberated from cyclic existence, and this is not sensible. Thinking of this Chandrakirti says in his *Supplement to the Middle Way* (*Madhyamakāvatāra*, VI. 131):

> According to you, a yogi who has seen selflessness
> Would not realise the suchness of forms and so forth.
> Thus desire and so forth would be generated
>   because of engaging in forms
> With apprehension [of inherent existence], for he
>   has not realised their nature.

Also, Chandrakirti's own commentary says, 'Because he has gone astray through apprehending an inherent existence of forms and so forth, he would not even realise the selflessness of persons. For he is apprehending [the inherent existence of] the mental and physical aggregates that are the cause of the imputation of a self.'

This is the thought of the protector Nagarjuna. His *Precious Garland* (*Ratnāvalī*, 35) says:

> As long as the aggregates are conceived,
> So long is there conception of an 'I'.
> When this conception of an 'I' exists,
> There is action which results in birth.

Also, Nagarjuna's *Treatise on the Middle Way* (*Madhyamakashāstra*, XVIII. 4–5) says:

> When actions and afflictions cease, there is
> liberation;
> They arise from false conceptions, these in turn
> arise
> From the elaborations [of false views on inherent
> Existence]; these elaborations cease in emptiness.

One is bound in cyclic existence through conceiving the aggregates to exist inherently, and in order to be liberated from that existence one must overcome its root, the elaborations of conceiving inherent existence. These are overcome through realising the meaning of the aggregates' emptiness of inherent existence. Also, Nagarjuna's *Praise of the Non-Conceptual (Nirvikalpastava [?])* says:

> The path of liberation relied upon
> By Buddhas, Solitary Realisers,
> And Hearers is only you,
> None other, it is definite.

Thus, Nagarjuna says that only the mother—the non-conceptual wisdom realising that phenomena do not inherently exist—is the path of liberation of all three vehicles. The *Mother of the Conquerors (The Eight Thousand Stanza Perfection of Wisdom Sutra, Aṣṭasāhasrikāprajñāpāramitā)*[15] says, 'Even one who wishes to train in the levels of a Hearer must train in just this perfection of wisdom.' The same was also said with respect to the levels of a Solitary Realiser and of a Buddha. The *Condensed Perfection of Wisdom Sutra (Sañchaya-gāthāprajñāpāramitā)*[16] states:

95

> Those who think to become Hearers of the Sugata
>   and those who wish
> To become Solitary Realisers or Kings of Doctrine
> Cannot achieve [their aims] without depending on
>   this endurance.

Nagarjuna collected together the meaning of these sutras. A Hearer scripture[17] says:

> Forms are like balls of foam.
> Feelings are like bubbles.
> Discriminations resemble mirages.
> Compositional factors are like banana tree trunks.
> Consciousnesses resemble magical illusions.
> Thus the Sun Friend Buddha said.

Indicating the same meaning, Nagarjuna's *Treatise on the Middle Way* (XV. 7) says:

> In the *Advice to Katyayana*
> 'Exists', 'does not exist', and 'both'
> Are rejected by the Blessed One who knows
> [The nature of][18] things and also non-things.

Thus, it is not that a selflessness of phenomena other than persons is not taught in the Hinayana scriptures.

However, in the Hearer scriptures there are many explanations that through the view of the sixteen attributes of the four truths—impermanence and so forth—one can reach the state of a Foe Destroyer. Also, in the Mahayana two modes of progress are taught—one through realisation that phenomena do not inherently exist and one through the paths of impermanence and so forth. Further, Mahayana sutras say that one can reach omniscience through both the Chittamatra and Madhyamika views. However, the master, the Superior Nagarjuna, showed in his *Collections of Reasoning*[19] that sutras teaching the

96

middle way were not suited to be understood differently and that, therefore, sutras illuminating the Chittamatra way must be interpreted otherwise. In the same way, here also such a system must be asserted.

The tantras also frequently say that Hearers and Solitary Realisers have not cognised the suchness of phenomena; however, it is also frequently stated that without cognising the suchness of phenomena one cannot leave cyclic existence and that thought conceiving the true existence of phenomena binds one in cyclic existence. Thus, you must know how to explain these without contradiction [through accepting as non-literal the teaching that Hearers and Solitary Realisers have not understood the suchness of phenomena].

Question: If the teachings of the paths of impermanence and so forth do not liberate one from cyclic existence, what is the purpose in teaching them?

Answer: Nagarjuna's *Sixty Stanzas of Reasoning (Yuktiṣhaṣhṭikā)* says:

> The paths of production and disintegration
> Were expounded for a meaningful purpose.
> Through knowing production one knows disintegration,
> Through knowing disintegration one knows
> impermanence.
> Through knowing impermanence
> One knows the excellent doctrine.
> Those who know how to abandon wholly
> The production and disintegration
> Of dependent-arisings cross the ocean
> Of cyclic existence with its [bad] views.

In this way you should know the purpose of teaching impermanence, for a mind thoroughly attracted to products does not wish to leave cyclic existence. As an

97

antidote, the paths of impermanence and suffering are taught, and thereby the wish to leave that existence arises. Then if one cognises—by way of the reason of production and disintegration—the excellent doctrine that dependent-arisings lack inherently existent production and disintegration, one will be liberated from cyclic existence. Thus, the path of liberation is only the realisation that persons and other phenomena do not inherently exist; the paths of impermanence and so forth are means of generating this realisation and also paths that train the mental continuum.

Other masters [Svatantrikas, Chittamatrins, Sautrantikas, and Vaibhashikas] do indeed assert that the paths of emptiness and selflessness are liberators and that cultivating the paths of the other aspects of the four truths, such as impermanence, trains the continuum for the sake of cognising selflessness. However, they identify the realisation of emptiness and selflessness among the sixteen aspects of the four truths as an ascertainment only that the self falsely imputed by non-Buddhists does not exist, and such realisation is not a suitable antidote to the innate conception that persons naturally exist. Thus, all the paths of the sixteen aspects are similar in not being liberating paths as well as in only being techniques to train the mental continuum.

A Hinayanist of dull faculties for the time being is a suitable vessel for paths that train the continuum, but not for a path that liberates. A Hinayanist of sharp faculties, however, is also suitable as a vessel of a path that liberates. The main or special trainees for whom Hinayana scriptures were spoken are the latter; the former are subsidiary trainees.

Even though Hinayanists realise that phenomena do not inherently exist, it is not that there is no difference between Hinayana and Mahayana. For the Mahayana teaching does not just clarify the selflessness of phenomena; it also presents the grounds, perfections, aspirational prayers, great compassion, dedications, two collections, and the inconceivable nature free from all defilements [a Buddha's Nature Body]. Nagarjuna's *Precious Garland* (390 and 393) says:

> Since all the aspirations, deeds and
> Dedications of Bodhisattvas
> Were not explained in the Hearers' vehicle, how then
> Could one become a Bodhisattva through its path?

> The subjects based on the deeds of Bodhisattvas
> Were not mentioned in the [Hinayana] sutras,
> But were explained in the Mahayana, thus the clear-
> Sighted should accept it [as the word of Buddha].

Hinayana and Mahayana are not differentiated through their view [of emptiness]; the Superior Nagarjuna and his sons assert that the two vehicles are discriminated by way of the acts of skilful method. For instance, a mother is a common cause of her children, but the fathers are the causes of discriminating their children's lineages [Tibetan, Mongolian, Indian, and so forth]. In the same way, the mother—the perfection of wisdom—is the common cause of all four sons [Hearer, Solitary Realiser, Bodhisattva, and Buddha Superiors], but the causes of their being divided into the individual lineages of Mahayana and Hinayana are methods, such as the generation of an aspiration to highest enlightenment for the sake of all sentient beings.

Presentation of Mahayana

Wishing to attain highest enlightenment for the sake of all sentient beings and consequently training in the Bodhisattva deeds—the six perfections—are the general meaning of being a follower of the Mahayana in the sense

99

of vehicle as the means by which one progresses. For it is said many times in tantras that in the Mantra Vehicle one proceeds by this path. However, within this context there are many distinctive attributes of the different paths.

The path of these persons is the Mahayana proceeding to omniscience, and the general body of the path is just this for Mahayanists of the Perfection Vehicle. However, when Mahayanists of the Perfection Vehicle are divided by way of their view of emptiness, there are Madhyamikas and Chittamatrins. Even so, they are not explained as having different vehicles; both are one vehicle. Since there is a difference of whether or not they have penetrated the depth of suchness, Madhyamikas are said to be of sharp faculties and Chittamatrins are said to be of dull faculties. Furthermore, Madhyamikas are the main special trainees for whom the Perfection Vehicle was taught; Chittamatrins are subsidiary or secondary trainees of that Vehicle.

Members of the Perfection Vehicle are said in the *Introduction to the Forms of Definite and Indefinite Progress Sutra (Niyatāniyatagatimudrāvatāra)*[20] to be of five types according to their speed on the path: two Bodhisattvas who progress carried respectively in an ox and an elephant chariot, one Bodhisattva borne by the moon and the sun, and two others by the magical creations of Hearers and Solitary Realisers or by the magical creations of Buddhas. Though they, like their examples, differ very greatly in their speed of progress on the path, they do not have individual vehicles. Therefore, the vehicles cannot be divided only by sharpness or dullness of faculty or by great or small progress.

Individual vehicles are posited (1) if there is a great difference of superiority or inferiority between them in the sense that a vehicle is a fruit or goal toward which one is progressing; or (2) if there are different stages of paths that give a different body to a vehicle in the sense that a vehicle is a cause by which one progresses. However, if the bodies

of the paths have no great difference in type, then a series
of vehicles cannot be assigned merely because the paths
have many internal divisions or the persons who progress
along them differ in superiority or inferiority.

All the Divisions Are Ultimately Branches of the Process of Fullest Enlightenment

Though Hinayanists do not engage in their own paths with
a view to attaining Buddhahood, their paths are methods
leading to Buddhahood. Therefore, it should not be strictly
held that Hinayana paths are obstacles to fullest
enlightenment. The *White Lotus of the Excellent Doctrine
(Saddharmapuṇḍarīka)* says:

> So that they might realize a Buddha's wisdom
> I taught these methods on my own.
> Still, I never said to them, 'You will become
>   Buddhas.'
> Why? The Protector sees the time.

Also:

> So that they might realise a Buddha's wisdom
> The sole Protector appears in the world.
> There is one vehicle, there are not two,
> Buddhas do not lead with a low vehicle.
> I set sentient beings in the powers,
> Concentrations, liberations, and forces,
> And paths like those in which a Buddha,
> An independent being, abides and realises.
> If, having realised the special pure enlightenment,
> I set some beings in a low vehicle, I would have
> The fault of miserliness, thus it would not be good.
> There is one vehicle, not two, never a third except
> For the various vehicles taught in the world
> Through the skilful means of superior beings.

The purpose of Buddha's coming to the world was for the sake of sentient beings' attaining the wisdom that he achieved. The paths that he taught are only means leading to Buddhahood; he does not lead sentient beings with a low vehicle that is not a method leading to Buddhahood. He establishes sentient beings in the powers and so forth that exist in his own state.

If, having attained enlightenment, he set some beings in a low vehicle that was not a means leading to Buddhahood, he would be miserly with respect to the doctrine. Since there is one final vehicle, those having a low lineage are also capable of being led to Buddhahood, and while knowing the methods to do that, he would have hidden from them the doctrines leading to Buddhahood in the sense that he would not teach these to them.

The *Chapter of the True One Sutra (Satyakaparivarta)* expresses it clearly:[21]

Manjushri, if the Tathagata taught Mahayana to some beings, the Solitary Realiser Vehicle to some, and the Hearer Vehicle to others, the Tathagata's mind would be very impure and without equanimity, with the fault of attraction, partial compassion and different discriminations. I would also then be miserly with regard to the doctrine.

Manjushri, all the doctrines that I teach to sentient beings are for the sake of attaining omniscient wisdom. Flowing into enlightenment and descending into the Mahayana, they are means of achieving omniscience, leading completely to one place. Therefore, I do not create different vehicles.

The meaning of 'If the Tathagata taught Mahayana to some ...' was explained above [on this page].

Question: Maitreya's *Ornament for the Mahayana Sutras* says:

If the intelligent live in a hell, it never
    interferes
With their [progress to] enlightenment broad and
    stainless.
Through a thought that takes delight in some
    other vehicle
One helps oneself and lives in happiness, but
    it interferes.

How should we take this statement that generating a
Hinayana attitude interferes [with attaining highest
enlightenment] and that being born in a hell does not?

Answer: There is no fault because this passage means that
if the intelligent—that is, Bodhisattvas—generate an
aspiration for Hinayana, they remove themselves far from
Buddhahood, but do not do so if they live in a hell. There is
no contradiction in the fact that for a Mahayanist Hinayana
is an obstacle to full enlightenment but for one in the
Hinayana lineage it is a method for full enlightenment.
Just previous to that stanza reference is made to Conqueror
Sons [Bodhisattvas]; therefore, the stanza is not a source
of debate [as it would be if the reference were to all
practitioners].

The *Compendium of All the Weaving Sutra
(Sarvavaidalyasaṃgraha)*[22] says that it would be an
abandonment of doctrine if one divided the Conqueror's
word into the good and the bad, the suitable and
unsuitable, or what is taught for Hearers and Solitary
Realisers and for Bodhisattvas. This refers to holding some of [Buddha's] words as methods for fullest enlightenment and some as obstacles to fullest
enlightenment.

In the same sutra[23] it is explained that if such
abandonment of doctrine occurs through a sinful guide,
the sin can be cleansed by confessing it three times a day
for seven years, but in order to attain endurance [the

103

facility to advance to the next level] one needs ten aeons. Thus, if time passes in wrong understanding, one is forced into great error. However, if unmistaken understanding [of the compatibility of the vehicles] is found, through merely finding it these faults [of abandonment of doctrine] do not occur.

You should understand that all doctrines taught by Buddha are, in relation to the trainees for whom they are taught, only methods leading to Buddhahood. In the same way the *Chapter of the True One Sutra* says that just as many rivers flow to a great ocean from different approaches, so all the water of the three vehicles flows into the great ocean of Tathagatahood. Still, it is correct that these methods differ in completeness and incompleteness and in the speed of their paths and so forth due to the superiority or inferiority of the trainees.

By reason of this, a path that is a part of the process leading to Buddhahood and a Mahayana path are not the same. Seeing the implications of this, the *Expression of the Ultimate Names of the Wisdom-Being Manjushri (Mañjushrījñānasattvasya paramārthanāmasaṃgīti)*[24] says:

> The deliverance of the three vehicles
> Abides in the fruit of the one vehicle.

Vajra Vehicle

Divisions of Mahayana

This section has two parts: division of Mahayana into two and a detailed explanation of the forms of entry to the Vajra Vehicle.

Division of Mahayana into Two

This section has three parts: the number of divisions of Mahayana, their meaning, and the reasons for them.

Number of Divisions of Mahayana

Shraddhakaravarma's *Introduction to the Meaning of Highest Yoga Tantras (Yogānuttaratantrārthāvatāra)*[25] says, 'There are two types of Bodhisattva vehicles, a [Cause] Vehicle of the grounds and perfections and an Effect Vehicle of Secret Mantra.' Thus, 'Secret Mantra Vehicle', 'Effect Vehicle', and 'Vajra Vehicle' are synonyms of the Mantra Vehicle, which is also called the 'Method Vehicle'. The term 'Cause-Effect Vehicle' is an enumeration of the two vehicles [of Perfection and Mantra]. The *Sutra Revealing the Secret*, as quoted in Jnanashri's *Eradication of the Two Extremes in the Vajra Vehicle (Vajrayānakoṭidvayāpoha)*,[26] says:

> Once the wheel of the cause doctrines
> Acting on the causes has been turned,
> The Effect Vehicle, the short path . . .

In the books of the Vajra Vehicle it is also known as the 'scriptural division of the Knowledge Bearers' and the 'sets of tantras'.

Meaning of the Individual Divisions of Mahayana
With respect to the 'Secret Mantra Vehicle', it is secret because it is achieved secretly and in hiding and is not taught to those who are not proper vessels for it. In the word 'mantra' *man* means mind and *tra [trā]* protection. The continuation of the *Guhyasamaja Tantra (Guhyasamājatantra*, chap. XVIII)[27] says:

> Minds arising dependent
> On a sense and an object
> Are said to be *man*,
> *Tra* means protection.

> Protection by means of all vajras
> Of the pledges and vows explained
> Free from the ways of the world
> Is called 'the practice of Mantra'.

You should know that in another way *man* is said to be knowledge of suchness and *trāya* to be compassion that protects those migrating [in the six types of cyclic existence].

About 'vehicle', there is an effect vehicle which is that to which one is proceeding and a cause vehicle which is that by which one proceeds. Due to proceeding [it is called] a vehicle. With respect to the 'Effect Vehicle', the word 'Effect' refers to the four thorough purities—abode, body, resources and deeds, which are a Buddha's palace, body, fortune and activities. In accordance with them one meditates on oneself as one presently having an inconceivable mansion, divine companions, sacred articles and deeds such as purification of environments and beings. Thus, it is called the 'Effect Vehicle' because one is progressing through meditation in accordance with the aspects of the effect [or fruit, Buddhahood]. Shraddhakaravarma's *Introduction to the Meaning of the Highest Yoga Tantras*[28] says, 'It is called "Effect" because one enacts the ways of thoroughly pure body, resources, abode and deeds.'

With respect to the 'Vajra Vehicle', the *Stainless Light (Vimālaprabhā)* [a commentary on the *Kalachakra Tantra* by Rik-den-pad-ma-kar-po (Rigs-ldan-pad-ma-dkar-po) an Emanation Body of Avalokiteshvara] says, ' "Vajra" means the indivisible and the great unbreakable. That is the Mahayana; this Mahayana is the Vajra Vehicle. It is a combination as one taste of the Mantra mode having the nature of the effect and the Perfection mode having the nature of the cause.' The meaning of 'Vajra Vehicle' is given through taking 'Vajra' as an indivisibility of the effect—the Mantra mode—and the cause—the Perfection mode. Here, 'cause and effect' refer to totally supreme emptiness and supreme immutable bliss. The *Brief Explication of Initiations (Shekhoddesha)* [included in the *Kalachakra* cycle] says:

> That bearing the form of emptiness is the cause,
> That bearing immutable compassion is the effect.
> Emptiness and compassion indivisible
> Are called the mind of enlightenment.

The indivisibility of these two is a Cause Vehicle in the sense of being the means by which one progresses, and it is an Effect Vehicle in the sense of being that to which one is progressing. Such a Vajra Vehicle has reference to Highest Yoga Tantra and cannot occur in the lower tantras. For the supreme immutable bliss can only arise when one has attained the branch of meditative stabilisation [in the system of the *Kalachakra*][29] and thus the branches of mindfulness and those below must be the means of achieving it. The three lower tantras do not have all the factors that are included in these causal branches.

Therefore, this interpretation of 'Vajra Vehicle' bears little relation to its general meaning, and the same applies to that of the meaning of the Vehicles of Cause and Effect. Here the meaning of 'Vajra Vehicle' should be taken in

107

accordance with what is said in Ratnakarashanti's *Handful of Flowers, Explanation of the Guhyasamaja Tantra (Kusumāñjaliguhyasamājanibandha)*: 'With regard to its being called the Vajra Vehicle, those which include all the Mahayana are the six perfections. Those that include them are method and wisdom; that which includes them as one taste is the mind of enlightenment. That is the Vajrasattva meditative stabilisation; just this is a vajra. Because it is both a vajra and a vehicle, it is the Vajra Vehicle, the Mantra Vehicle.' Thus, the Vajrasattva yoga that indivisibly unites method and wisdom is the Vajra Vehicle. It occurs at the time of both the path and the fruit.

Because the Vajra Vehicle has more skilful means than that of the Perfections, it is called the Method Vehicle. Jnanashri's *Eradication of the Two Extremes*[30] says, 'Because of indivisibility, it is the Vajra Vehicle. Because just the effect becomes the path, it is the Effect Vehicle. Because of the greatness of its methods, it is the Method Vehicle. Because of its extreme secrecy, it is the Secret Vehicle.'

'Scriptural division of the Knowledge Bearers' should be taken as referring to teaching the topics of training and the tenets of those who bear the knowledge mantras. It is explained in this way in Buddhaguhya's *Condensation of the Questions of Subahu Tantra (Subāhupariprchchhānāmatantrapiṇḍārtha)*. Shraddhakaravarma explains it in two ways in his *Introduction to the Meaning of the Highest Yoga Tantras*:[31] one in which the scriptural division of the Knowledge Bearers is a fourth scriptural division not included in the three scriptural divisions [discipline, sets of discourses, and knowledge] and one in which it is included in the three scriptural divisions. However, the *Questions of Subahu Tantra (Subāhupariprchchhā)* says, 'Listen, I will explain this in accordance with the sets of discourses of Secret Mantra.' Also, in many tantras 'sutras' and 'sets of discourses' are mentioned [in reference to tantra]. Therefore, Ratnakarashanti rightly asserts that this 'scriptural division' is the 'sets of discourses' *(sūtrānta)* because they teach profound meanings in abridged form. However, if the scriptural division of the Knowledge Bearers is considered in terms of its internal divisions, it also teaches meanings of the other scriptural divisions [discipline and knowledge]; therefore, Abhayakara's assertion that the scriptural division of the Knowledge Bearers is included in all three scriptural divisions is also correct.

In the continuation of the *Guhyasamaja Tantra*[32] 'tantra' is said to mean 'continuum' and to be of three types: a 'base continuum' that is the base on which the paths are acting [to purify it of obstructions], a 'path continuum' that purifies this base, and a 'fruit continuum' that is the fruit of purification. All three are tantras in the sense of being objects of discussion [in books called tantras]. A scripture taking any of these as its object of discussion is a 'book continuum' [tantra] discussing [such subjects].

The word 'set' in 'sets of tantras' *(tantrānta)* means a collection or group of tantras.

The Perfection Vehicle has as the basis of its practices the generation of an aspiration to highest enlightenment for the sake of all sentient beings. It proceeds by way of its practices, the six perfections, and does not have other paths such as the two stages [of Highest Yoga Tantra]. If the Perfection Vehicle were taken just as that which involves generation of an aspiration to highest enlightenment for the sake of all sentient beings and proceeds by way of the six perfections [without qualifying that it does not have paths such as the two stages], then the Vajra Vehicle would also be a Perfection Vehicle.

The Perfection Vehicle is called the Cause Vehicle because it does not include cultivation of a path that

109

accords in aspect with the four fruits mentioned earlier
[abode, body, resources and activities of a Buddha] and
has only meditation on their causes.

Reasons for Division of Mahayana into a
Perfection Vehicle and a Vajra Vehicle

This section has two parts: the statement of points
generating doubts in the discriminative and an answer.

Statement of Points Generating Doubts in the
Discriminative

Why is Mahayana divided into two vehicles? It is not from
the viewpoint of generating an aspiration to highest
enlightenment for the sake of all sentient beings. For
Bodhisattvas equally practise by way of Mantra and the
Perfection Vehicle in order to attain perfect Buddhahood
for the sake of all sentient beings. There is also no
difference of superiority and inferiority in the
enlightenment that they seek for this purpose; thus, the
Mahayana cannot be divided into two vehicles from the
viewpoint of the enlightenment sought.

The division is not about whether or not it has the view
cognising the suchness of phenomena. For there is no view
superior to Nagarjuna's presentation in his *Treatise on the
Middle Way* of the thought of the definitive sutras, such as
the *Perfection of Wisdom Sutras.* Even if there were a
superior view, it could not establish the existence of
individual vehicles—similarly, though the Perfection
Vehicle has Madhyamika and Chittamatra, these two are
not individual vehicles.

Also, practice of the six perfections occurs in both the
Perfection and Vajra Vehicles. Thus, there is no difference
with respect to the main paths—method and wisdom—for
achieving the Form and Truth Bodies of a Buddha.

Though the Vajra Vehicle does have some features of paths that do not exist in the Perfection Vehicle, these are not features of the main paths; therefore, such differences cannot establish the existence of separate vehicles.

Also, the mere existence of a difference of sharpness or dullness of faculties in persons [who train in these paths] or in the speed of progress on the paths cannot establish separate vehicles, just as the Perfection Vehicle does not have separate vehicles even though it has such differences. Otherwise, many of these would have to be assigned within the Mantra Vehicle itself.

Answer

The answer is in two parts: refutation of others' positions and presentation of the correct position.

Refutation of Others' Positions on the Reason for Dividing Mahayana into Perfection and Vajra Vehicles

Some say, 'Mantra was propounded for the sake of taming desirous trainees, and the Perfection Vehicle for the sake of training trainees free from desire. Therefore, cultivation of a path without abandoning desire or of a path that abandons desire is the reason dividing the Mahayana into two vehicles.'

I will explain this. [It is wrong to say that] Mahayana is divided into two vehicles because the respective trainees cultivate a path without abandoning desire or a path that abandons desire. For, since both vehicles have both paths, this feature cannot distinguish the vehicles. There are many householder Bodhisattvas who engage in the paths of the Perfection Vehicle but have not abandoned impure deeds. Also, there are many skilled in method who out of great altruism act impurely, as in the case of the Brahmin Kyiu-kar-ma (Khyi'u-skar-ma). Also, among the trainees of the Mantra Vehicle there are many who have abandoned attachment to the attributes of the desire realm. Otherwise, there would be the fault that one could not be freed from the desires of that realm until Buddhahood, or that, having attained Buddhahood, one would still not have abandoned these.

Objection: This is not to be applied to any and all trainees of the Mantra and Perfection Vehicles. It is to be taken within the framework of the special or main trainees who are initially entering these paths. Furthermore, a trainee of the Mantra Vehicle is not just someone who is suitable for cultivating the paths of that vehicle without having intentionally abandoned desire for the attributes of the desire realm. Whether someone is or is not a trainee of the Mantra Vehicle is determined by whether or not one has the good fortune [of having formerly accumulated meritorious actions] such that desire can become a cause of liberation through its being able to act as an aid in the path.

Answer: As will be explained later,[33] the *Samputa Tantra (Saṃpuṭatantra)* indeed says:

> The four aspects of laughing, looking,
> Holding hands and the two embracing
> Reside as the four tantras
> In the manner of insects.

Therefore, we must assert that the trainees of the four tantras each use pleasure in the path in dependence on four types of desire for the attributes of the desire realm [looking, laughing, holding hands, and union. The presence or absence of such an ability to use pleasure in the path] is suitable as a difference between persons who are initially entering the Mantra or Perfection Vehicles; however, such cannot distinguish the vehicles.

Similarly, Mahayana cannot be divided into a Mantra

and a Perfection Vehicle through whether or not their paths are adorned with bliss or concentration occurs on essential points in the body and mind. 'Adornment with bliss' might be taken to mean that through cultivating the path a special bliss arises in the body and a special joy in the mind, so that the mind abides steadily on its object. However, Asanga says in his *Treatises on the Levels* that for all those who initially achieve calm abiding, first a physical wind becomes pliant whereby a great bliss arises in the body and, in turn, a special joy arises in the mind. In dependence on this, the mind calmly abides on its object. Therefore, special physical bliss and special mental joy exist in calm abiding, whether one be a Buddhist or not. How, then, could these determine the division of the paths into Mantra and Perfection Vehicles? Since I have explained this extensively in my *Stages of the Path Common to the Vehicles*, I will not elaborate on it here.

Objection: 'Adornment with bliss' refers to a cognition of the meaning of suchness in dependence on a 'melting bliss' which in turn depends on precepts for achieving the special essential of the meeting and staying together of the white and red minds of enlightenment.[34]

Answer: This is not suitable for establishing the difference between the general Vajra and Perfection Vehicles because it is a feature only of Highest Mantra [Highest Yoga Tantra]. For the same reason, it should be understood that concentration on essential points in the mind and body is not suitable to be the difference between the two vehicles.

Presentation of the Correct Position on Dividing Mahayana into Perfection and Mantra Vehicles

This section has two parts: the actual reason for dividing Mahayana into two vehicles and a teaching that though the

113

paths have differences their fruits do not differ as to superiority and inferiority.

Actual Reason for Dividing Mahayana into Perfection and Mantra Vehicles

This section has three parts: reason for the division, citing sources, and dispelling objections.

Reason for Dividing Mahayana into Perfection and Mantra Vehicles

With regard to 'vehicle' in the sense of being the fruit to which trainees progress, the Mantra and Perfection Vehicles do not differ as to superiority or inferiority. The object of attainment for both paths is the Buddhahood that is a removal of all faults and a completion of all auspicious attributes. Therefore, the two differ with respect to the sense of 'vehicle' as the causes by which trainees progress.

Furthermore, there is no difference in their realisation (the view [of emptiness]), their thought (generation of an aspiration to highest enlightenment for the sake of all sentient beings), or their behaviour (mere training in the six perfections). Therefore, the Vehicles as causes cannot be divided from these points of view.

Question: From what viewpoint are they divided?

Answer: The chief aims sought by both types of Mahayanists are those of others, not the enlightenment that is the aim of one's own attainment. For, seeing Buddhahood as a means to achieve others' aims, they seek highest enlightenment as a branch of the aims of others. Maitreya's *Ornament for the Realisations (Abhisamayālamkāra)* says:

> Mind generation is the wish for complete
> Perfect enlightenment for the sake of others.

Altruistic mind generation is similar for both types of Mahayanists.

A Buddha who actually appears to trainees and achieves their aims is not the Truth Body but the two aspects of the Form Body [the Bodies of Complete Enjoyment and Emanation]. A Truth Body is achieved through the wisdom cognising the profound [emptiness] and Form Bodies are achieved through vast methods. Also, the Two Bodies cannot be attained with a wisdom lacking method or with a method lacking wisdom. Therefore, one needs inseparable wisdom and method; this is a tenet of Mahayanists in general.

Without cognising the mode of subsistence of phenomena, one cannot extinguish all afflictions and cross to the other side of the ocean of cyclic existence. Therefore, the wisdom cognising the profound [emptiness] is even common to the two lower types of Superiors [Hearers and Solitary Realisers].

Thus, the main distinctive feature of the Mahayana paths must be taken as the methods serving as the causes of becoming a protector and refuge for sentient beings as long as cyclic existence lasts, through appearing in Form Bodies to fortunate trainees. Those of the Perfection Vehicle cultivate paths that accord in aspect with the Truth Body through meditating on the suchness of phenomena free of the elaborations [of conventionalities, duality and conception of inherent existence]. However, they do not have paths of meditation that are similar in aspect to a Form Body adorned with the major and minor marks whereas Mantra does. Thus, there is a great difference in the corpus of the Perfection and Mantra paths with respect to the method for achieving Form Bodies in order to achieve the welfare of others. It is by this method that Mahayana is divided into two vehicles.

For, in general, one must divide Hinayana and Mahayana not by the wisdom of emptiness but by method, and in particular the division of the Mahayana into two is not made on account of the wisdom cognising the profound emptiness but on account of method. The chief method is taken from the viewpoint of the achievement of Form Bodies, for which Mantra's deity yoga—meditation on oneself as having an aspect similar to a Form Body—is superior to the method of the Perfection Vehicle.

Deity Yoga

Citing Sources

This section has two parts: how the method is explained in the texts of Highest Yoga and in those of the lower tantras.

How the Method is Explained in the Texts of Highest Yoga

This section has two parts: how the method is explained in tantras and in commentaries.

How the Method is Explained in Highest Yoga Tantras

The first chapter of the *Vajrapanjara Tantra (Vajrapañjara)*[35] expresses the method clearly:

> If emptiness were the method, then
> Buddhahood could not be. Since other
> Than this cause there would be no other fruit,
> The method is not emptiness.
>
> The Conquerors teach emptiness
> To overcome the conceptions of self
> In those who from [right] views have turned away
> And in those who seek the view of self.
>
> Therefore it is the 'circle of a mandala',
> It is a binding of the blissful method.
> Through the yoga of Buddha pride
> Buddhahood will not be distant.
>
> A Teacher has the two and thirty signs
> As well as all the eighty minor marks,
> Therefore the method of achievement
> Is to take on the Teacher's form.

117

One by one these four stanzas (1) refute the assertion that merely meditating on emptiness is the method, and indicate (2) the purpose of teaching emptiness, (3) the uncommon method and its greatness, and (4) the reason why Buddhahood is achieved through this method.

The first stanza means: It was taught earlier in the *Vajrapanjara* that, since the mind is polluted with the taints of one's own thoughts, one should make every effort to purify it. Then one might think, 'To cleanse these taints, one should meditate only on emptiness because the wisdom cognising the suchness of selflessness is opposed to thoughts conceiving self [inherent existence] whereas other paths do not contradict these thoughts. Therefore, the method for developing into a Buddha is only meditation on emptiness. Of what use are other elaborations?'

It is said that no matter how hard one works at such a method, one cannot become a Buddha. For, except a cause which is a meditation on emptiness, there would be no method [to achieve] the fruit [of Buddhahood]; since the branch of method would be lacking, the causes would not be complete. Thus, to gain familiarity only with emptiness is not a complete method. Devakulamahamati's explanation[36] is good, that this is the system not only of Mantra but also of the Perfection Vehicle.

Question: Then what is the purpose of teaching emptiness?

Answer: Emptiness, or selflessness, was taught for the sake of overcoming the two conceptions of self in those who have turned away from the views of the selflessness of phenomena and so forth and in those who seek the view of a self [of persons] in the sense that they strongly adhere to a conception of it. This shows that in order to cleanse the taints of thoughts of the two types of self [inherent existence both of persons and of phenomena] one definitely must seek and cultivate a viewing consciousness cognising suchness—selflessness.

It is similarly taught in the Perfection Vehicle that meditation only on emptiness is insufficient and that its purpose is to cleanse the mind. This explanation of the two lines 'In those who from [right] views have turned away/ And in those who seek the view of self,' accords with the thought of Devakulamahamati's commentary on the *Vajrapanjara.*

Question: If mere meditation on emptiness is not a complete method, what is the special one?

Answer: Because mere meditation on emptiness is not feasible as the method, the special one is 'the circle of a mandala' [a 'resident mandala' which is a divine body and a 'residence mandala' which is the deity's abode]. This is how the stanzas should be connected.

In Devakulamahamati's commentary to the *Vajrapanjara*[37] the next line is translated [into Tibetan] as 'The method is a blissful binding.' This is a better translation than the one given above, 'It is a binding of the blissful method'. Here, a method superior to that of the Perfection Vehicle is being indicated, and it has been shown that mere meditation on emptiness is not a complete method. Thus, there is a method to be added to meditation on emptiness, and it is said to be deity yoga. Thereby, meditation on a mandala circle [divine resident and residence] is known to be the main method for [achieving] a Form Body.

The features of this method are two, blissfulness and binding. Blissfulness is non-dependence on asceticism. Many modes of binding are put forth in the *Hevajra Tantra,* but at this point binding should be understood as an indivisibility of method—the appearance of a divine circle—and wisdom—cognition of the emptiness of inherent existence.

119

With such a yoga of method and wisdom in which one cultivates the pride of a Buddha such as Vairochana, one attains the state of a Buddha without the passage of a long time as in the Perfection Vehicle. In this way the greatness of the Mantra path is presented. The explanation that deity yoga is the quick path refutes wrong ideas that deity yoga is useless for achieving the supreme.

Question: Why is it that in order to achieve a Form Body one needs a yoga bearing the pride of a Buddha and the aspect of a mandala circle?

Answer: The *Vajrapanjara* says:

> A Teacher has the two and thirty signs
> As well as all the eighty minor marks,
> Therefore the method of achievement
> Is to take on the Teacher's form.

Taking as the reason that a Form Body—the object of attainment—is adorned with the major and minor marks, it is said that the fruit must be achieved through a method which has the form or aspect of a Teacher.

In the other two commentaries on the *Vajrapanjara* [by Krshnapada[38] and by Indrabodhi[39]] it does not appear that doubts are eradicated and that the topic is clearly explained, but such is done in Devakulamahamati's commentary[40] [even though not all of it is correct]. In his commentary on the first stanza, at the point of refuting that mere meditation on emptiness is the method, he explains that if one cultivated only an emptiness lacking method, one would be born in an unfortunate existence such as in Limitless Space. This is not correct [because one would become a Hinayana Foe Destroyer].

Then, in answer to the theory that at the time of the path emptiness is the method and at the time of maturation emptiness is the fruit, Devakulamahamati explains that since the emptiness both of the cause or path and of the effect or maturation would have no other distinctive features, emptiness—while it was being asserted as the effect—could not also be the method. He adds that since the cause is an elaborative entity involving apprehension [of inherent existence] and the effect is the opposite, the cause and the effect are different; therefore, the method is not just emptiness.

His explanation of the purpose for teaching emptiness is the same as that given above. Then, there is the doubt 'If it is taught in the Perfection Vehicle that enlightenment is achieved through the practice—for three countless aeons—of the perfection of wisdom conjoined with the other five perfections, what is the use of methods such as a mandala circle?' To eliminate this doubt Devakulamahamati explains the blissfulness in the third stanza as it was above. He says that 'binding' is to experience the bliss of the union of the two organs [which is limited to Highest Yoga Tantra]. The 'pride of being a Buddha' he [correctly] explains as being free from the pride of ordinariness, and 'not be distant' he explains as attaining Buddhahood in this life [but this is also limited to Highest Yoga Tantra].

One might think that a Buddha Body is to be cultivated in the mode of a Truth Body [in meditative equipoise on emptiness alone]. The last stanza eliminates this qualm; Devakulamahamati explains that the method is the three meditative stabilisations in the form of the Three Bodies.

Many Tibetan lamas have [wrongly] applied the teaching of deity yoga—a mandala circle—only to the first stage of Highest Yoga Tantra [that of generation]. This has the fault of not discriminating between the respective greater and lesser extent of deity yoga [which occurs in the three lower tantras and both stages of Highest Yoga] and the stage of generation [which occurs only in Highest

Yoga and is the first of two stages]. Deity yoga should be taken as applicable to both stages [generation and completion].

This conception that meditation on emptiness is the only means for achieving both Bodies is the greater basis of wrong ideas that omit deity yoga as a method for the supreme achievement [Buddhahood]. I have quoted the *Vajrapanjara* because it clearly eliminates this doubt and clearly says that deity yoga must be cultivated as a cause of a Form Body. Thus, with this as an illustration, the teachings of the other tantras should be understood. Fearing it would be too much, I will not cite them here.

How the Method is Explained in Highest Yoga Commentaries

This section has two parts: how the method is explained in the master Jnanapada's texts and then by other masters.

How the Method is Explained in the Master Jnanapada's Texts

The teacher Jnanapada sets forth a very clear exposition of what is taught in the tantra quoted above in his *Engaging in the Means of Self-Achievement (Ātmasādhanāvatāra).* First he sets forth the way of the Perfection Vehicle,[41] saying:

> If meditation on selflessness lacks the features of method, it cannot generate an omniscient wisdom free from all taints of thought and aiding all migrators. Therefore, one should work hard at a very clear method. For that which has a nature of helping all beings is an omniscient wisdom, and this help arises from the ultimate vastness, its cause being only the cultivation of method because cultivation of selflessness has the fruit

of only forsaking thought. Further, [Maitreya's *Ornament for the Mahayana Sutras*] says:

Because of profundity and because of vastness
These two [wisdom and method] are taught for the two,
Non-conceptuality and full maturation,
Therefore, they are the highest method of all.

Non-perverse activities of mind, such as giving and so forth, are the method because when they are thoroughly dedicated to omniscient wisdom they become the causes of complete enlightenment. [The *Condensed Perfection of Wisdom Sutra*] says:

Thoroughly dedicate to enlightenment giving,
Ethics, patience, effort, concentration, and wisdom.
Hold not enlightenment to be supreme adhering
To it as a mass.[42] Such is taught to beginners.

By this Jnanapada means: If one lacks the vast method, no matter how much one meditates on selflessness, one cannot attain Buddhahood which sustains all migrators. Therefore, one must work hard at method. The state helping all sentient beings is the imprint [result] only of the vast method because the imprint of meditation on selflessness is an abandonment—only an extinguishing of taints.

This does not teach that through meditation on emptiness, without the vast method, one can extinguish all taints but cannot bring about the welfare of all sentient beings. Nor does it teach that through cultivating only the vast method without meditation on emptiness one can attain a Form Body that brings about the welfare of all sentient beings, but cannot attain a Truth Body—which is an extinguishment of all taints. For neither Body can be attained without the other. Since Truth and Form Bodies have the definite relation of depending on one causal collection, they are never separated.

Moreover, the wisdom cognising emptiness, which is impelled by the precious aspiration to enlightenment for the sake of all sentient beings, purifies all the taints of conceiving self. Therefore, this wisdom is the special cause of a Truth Body that possesses the two purities [natural purity and purity from adventitious stains]. However, the wisdom cognising emptiness is also a co-operative cause of a Form Body.

Similarly, the vast methods are the special causes of a Form Body but also the co-operative causes of a Truth Body. For, if one does not work hard at these methods, no matter how much one meditates on the suchness of phenomena, one can only leave cyclic existence and cannot arrive at a Truth Body which is an extinguishment of all taints. Also, if one does not strive for the wisdom cognising emptiness, no matter how much one works at these methods, one cannot arrive at a Form Body.

Nevertheless, the extinguishment of all taints upon becoming a Buddha must be taken as an imprint of having meditated on emptiness, whereas becoming the sustenance of all migrators must be taken as the imprint of the vast methods. For example, since all three conditions must be present to produce an eye consciousness apprehending blue, that consciousness is an effect of all three. However, its apprehension of a visible form and not other objects, such as sounds, is an imprint of the eye sense. Its being generated as an experiential entity is the imprint of the 'immediately preceding condition' [a former moment of consciousness]. Its being generated in the image of blue is the imprint of the object.

The quote from Maitreya's *Ornament for the Mahayana Sutras* [on page 123] is a source showing that if both factors of method and wisdom are complete, they are the unsurpassed method for achieving the fruit. The quote from the *Condensed Perfection of Wisdom Sutra* [on page 123] is a source showing that if the methods for achieving Buddhahood—giving and so forth—are dedicated to enlightenment and conjoined with the wisdom of non-apprehension [of inherent existence], they become [actual] methods [capable of causing attainment of Buddhahood].

After that, Jnanapada sets forth the special method of the Mantra Vehicle:[43] 'That is not so in fact because aside from cultivating different causes there is no meditation that accords with actualised complete enlightenment.' This means that giving and so forth, which in the Perfection Vehicle are explained as the method, are not the unsurpassed or highest method because they lack the meditation that accords in aspect with an actualised Buddha Body. For in the Perfection Vehicle one only cultivates paths completely different in aspect from the fruit [of a Form Body].

Jnanapada proves that if [a system] has no cultivation of a path that accords in aspect with a Form Body, it is not an unsurpassed method for achieving Buddhahood. He says,[44] 'The fruits that by their own entity have a nature of profundity and vastness are achieved from their own nature.'

Thus, in general the fruits to be attained are a Truth Body with a nature of profundity and [a Form Body] adorned with the major and minor marks with a nature of vastness. Further, the wisdom mind abides as one taste with the suchness of phenomena and never rises from it, while the body, adorned with the flaming major and minor marks, abides without ever changing. These two are undifferentiable in one entity; this is the meaning of 'by their own entity'. Thus, the method and wisdom that achieve such [results] must accord with them. For example, when [practising to] achieve the mind of a Conqueror—a Truth Body—a yogi places his mind now in the suchness of phenomena and cultivates a path that accords in aspect with the mind of a Conqueror. In the same way, when [practising to] achieve a Form Body, a yogi must cultivate a path that accords in aspect with that Body in the sense that his own body appears to have the major and minor marks. For, a Truth and a Form Body are thoroughly similar in the sense that if the one path of similar aspect is practised, the other should be practised, and if the one is omitted, the other should be omitted.

Thinking of this, Jnanapada says in his *Self-Achievement*,[45] 'Therefore, as in the case with selflessness one should meditate on the nature of vastness in the mode of non-difference.' The vastness of this system is deity yoga; I will explain later [in the section on Highest Yoga Tantra] how it is vast. Achievement through such means is called 'achievement from their own nature'.

At the time of the fruit, the base—a body adorned with the major and minor marks—and the mind of non-apprehension [of inherent existence] which depends on it abide at one time as an undifferentiable entity. In the same way, at the time of the path, the method is that the yogi's body appears to his own mind in the aspect of a Tathagata's body, and at the same time his mind becomes the wisdom apprehending suchness—the non-inherent existence of all phenomena. These two are a simultaneous composite, undifferentiable in the entity of one consciousness. This should be understood as [the meaning of] undifferentiable method and wisdom [in the Mantra Vehicle]. Through cultivating the yoga of joining these two at the same time one attains the state in which non-dualistic wisdom itself appears as Form Bodies to trainees.

If the supreme method—the appearance of a deity—is devoid of wisdom and bereft of the unmistaken cognition of the nature of one's own mind, one cannot progress to Buddhahood. Therefore, it is necessary to have a composite of the two. Jnanapada's *Self-Achievement*[46] says, 'Since a Subduer having immeasurable effulgence of light serves as a source of limitless marvels for oneself and others, even if this which has the character of being the supreme right method were manifestly cultivated but bereft of wisdom, it would not be a means of achieving all marvels; therefore, the nature [of the divine body] should be known without mistake'.

The wisdom cognising non-inherent existence and appearing in the aspect of a deity is itself one entity with the mind of deity yoga, the vast. However, method and wisdom are presented as different by force of the convention of different opposites of negatives in dependence on the fact that their opposites are different. Wisdom is established from the viewpoint of being the opposite of a mind that mistakenly conceives the meaning of suchness. For knowledge of the ultimate [emptiness]—the final object of knowledge—is the supreme knowledge. Method is established from the viewpoint of being the opposite of that which does not have the capacity of achieving its fruit, Buddhahood. For the methods of Buddhahood are capable of achieving that state. In this way Jnanapada's *Self-Achievement*[47] says, 'Also, these [method and wisdom] are one nature in the unmistaken vast mind. Even so, the convention of difference causes one to understand that they are different. It is thus: Wisdom is known by way of its being an entity that is the opposite of a mind mistaken about suchness, and method is shown to be that which is the opposite of not being able to bear its respective fruit.' Even though Jnanapada describes the procedure of establishing method and wisdom in a general way, at this point the bases [he uses] for positing method and wisdom are the special method and wisdom of Mantra.

Thus, a Form Body is achieved through the appearance of the wisdom apprehending [emptiness] as a divine

127

mandala circle, and a Truth Body is achieved through the cognition of its nature—emptiness. One should know that joining such method and wisdom non-dualistically is the chief meaning of the method and wisdom and of the yogas set forth in the Mantra Vehicle.

Method in the Four Tantras

How the Method is Explained
by Other Masters of Highest Yoga

Ratnakarashanti's *Commentary on (Dipankarabhadra's) 'Four Hundred and Fifty' (Guhyasamājamaṇḍalavidhi-ṭīkā)*[48] says, 'If one cultivates only [a path] having the nature of a deity, one cannot become fully enlightened merely through that because the fulfilment of [yogic] activities is not complete. Or, if one meditates on the suchness of a deity and not on that deity, one will attain Buddhahood in many countless aeons but not quickly. Through meditating on both, one will attain the highest perfect complete enlightenment very quickly because to do so is very appropriate and has special empowering blessings.'

Thus, Ratnakarashanti says that if one cultivates only deity yoga, one simply cannot become fully enlightened. Also, even if one does not meditate on a deity, through meditation on emptiness accompanied by other methods one can become fully enlightened in many countless aeons. If one meditates both on a deity and on emptiness, it is the quick path.

Therefore, the master Ratnakarashanti also asserts that the view of emptiness is common to both Mahayanas and that without deity yoga the path is slow like the Perfection Vehicle, but through joining deity yoga with the view of emptiness the path is quick. Ratnakarashanti is following the explanation above [in the *Vajrapanjara* and the *Self-Achievement*].

Abhayakara explains the method in accordance with Ratnakarashanti in the eighteenth cluster of *Clusters of*

129

Quintessential Instructions(Āmnāyamañjari)[49] and quotes as a source the fourteenth chapter of the *Vajrapanjara*:[50]

> To overcome pride of ordinariness
> This meditation is known to be perfect.

Also: 'For the sake of purifying the unclean body one should meditate on a Buddha Body.'[51]

Durjayachandra in his commentary on the first chapter of the *Hevajra Tantra* quotes the first and fourteenth chapters of the *Vajrapanjara* and explains that causes cannot achieve an effect that is not concordant with them. Shridhara, in his *Innate Illumination, Commentary on the Difficult Points of the Yamari Tantra (Yamāritantrapañjikāsahajāloka)*,[52] says:

> It should not be said that [Form Bodies] will arise through methods, such as giving and so forth, and by the power of prayer petitions. How could one who hesitates about those having the nature of complete enjoyment [an Enjoyment Body] and emanation [an Emanation Body] which are not being meditated on become firm in mind [about them]?
>
> One might think, 'Still, these will arise by the power of prayer-petitions.' Then, without having meditated on selflessness, [a Truth Body] could become manifest [which is absurd]; what would be the use of the hard work of meditating on selflessness?
>
> One might think, '[A Truth Body] arises from meditation.' Then what is wrong with a Complete Enjoyment and an Emanation Body? Why should one not meditate on them? Even those abiding in the Perfection Vehicle assert a Buddhahood having an essence of the Three Bodies. Through meditation on them they are manifested.

If one meditates on selflessness which has the aspect of a Truth Body, one must also do so on a deity which has the aspect of a Form Body. If one does not, it is the same as asserting that without meditating on selflessness, a Truth Body can be actualised.

As a source for this Shridhara[53] quotes:

> The cause of achieving Buddhahood
> Is Buddha yoga. Is it not seen
> Truly that in all ways cause
> And effect are similar?

He also quotes the *All Secret (Sarvarahasya,* a Yoga Tantra):[54]

> In brief Buddhahood definitely
> Arises from stabilisation
> And wisdom. Without Buddha yoga
> A yogi attains not Buddhahood.

Samayavajra explains it similarly in his *Commentary on the Krshnayamari Tantra (Kṛṣhṇayamāritantrarājaṭīkā),*[55] as does Jinadatta in his *Commentary on the Difficult Points of the Guhyasamaja Tantra (Guhyasamājatantrapañjikā).*[56]

Vinayadatta explains the method at length in his *Rite of the Great Illusion Mandala (Mahāmāyāmaṇḍalopāyika):*[57] 'This meaning was spoken by the honorable guru himself:

> Meditating that one is both a Form and Truth Body,
> O, enlightenment is definitely attained.
> If through a Conqueror's concentration a Truth
>   Body is gained,
> Why is a Form Body not meditated upon?
>
> Though a Form Body is attained through collecting
>   merit,
> That takes long and is thus lower than the other.
> From causes having the features of their effects
> The Three Bodies simultaneously appear.'

Though there are many other sources in treatises, I have cited these because they are clear.

How the Method is Explained
in the Texts of the Lower Tantras

In his *Self-Achievement* [a Highest Yoga text] Jnanapada says that the vast deity yoga constitutes the difference in method between the Perfection and Mantra Vehicles. He proves this by citing a passage on deity generation by way of the [five] clarifications in [the Yoga Tantra] *Compendium of Principles (Tattvasaṃgraha)*. He also clearly explains how the deities of the vajra element [a topic distinctive to Yoga Tantra] are all involved in this yoga.[58] Therefore, he asserts, deity yoga is a feature of the method not only of Highest Yoga but also of Yoga Tantra.

Though other masters likewise explain deity yoga when dealing with Highest Yoga Tantra, it [actually] is similar in all the sets of tantras in which one generates oneself in the aspect of a deity. This is because the reasons for having to meditate thus are similar.

Moreover, deity yoga is frequently mentioned in Yoga Tantras. The first section of the *Compendium of Principles*[59] says:

> If one meditates on a Buddha Body
> With one's own fine particles
> Of body, speech and mind as vajras
> One will become a complete Buddha.

On this Shakyamitra's *Ornament of Kosala (Kosalālaṃkā-ratattvasaṃgrahaṭīkā)* comments, 'This means four meditative sessions each day on a Buddha Body by way of the disciplinary yoga of mental application; one meditates on one's finest particles as vajras and so forth. What feat will be the result of meditating on oneself as having a Buddha Body? The text says, "One will become a complete Buddha." This means that one will attain a Buddha Body adorned with the major and minor marks.'

Also, Anandagarbha's commentary on the first part of the *Compendium of Principles* called *Illumination of Principles (Tattvāloka)*[60] states, '[This was said] in order to indicate that those practising the approach of Secret Mantra should cultivate mindfulness of a Buddha. They should be mindful of a Form Body and the final nature of a Tathagata.' Also, 'One should maintain an abiding in the centre of all Tathagatas; one should meditate [on oneself] in the manner of a Truth Body and a Form Body conjoined with [a Buddha], not of different nature but undifferentiable, until one has vividly seen oneself [as a Buddha].'

Since it is very clear that a Truth Body is achieved by the wisdom cognising emptiness, I will not cite any sources.

The way that deity yoga is put forth in the texts of Action and Performance Tantras is as follows. Buddhaguhya's *Condensation of the Vairochanabhisambodhi (Vairochanābhisaṃbodhitantrapiṇḍārtha)* says, 'In accordance with the order of [yoga] both with and without signs, the entities of divine bodies are taught as two types from the viewpoint of thoroughly impure and pure bodies. The thoroughly pure is the entity of the signless meditative stabilisation on a Truth Body having the nature of aspectless wisdom. The thoroughly impure are entities of imputed forms, having the character of the Buddhas' Bodies of Complete Enjoyment and Emanation and with the colour and shape necessary for appearing to beings who are trainees.' Thus, two yogas—meditations in accordance with the aspects of the Two Bodies—are taught. This is similar in both Action and Performance Tantras.

Though the two Mahayanas are neither superior nor

133

inferior with respect to view, they are divided here by way of the vast—deity yoga. This is clearly stated in Ratnakarashanti's *Presentation of the Three Vehicles (Triyānavyavasthāna)*:[61] 'There is no second ultimate truth superior to the ultimate truth presented by the Blessed One, Nagarjuna, and so forth. Through mere conventionalities how could it become more vast?

> Because of a very pure object,
> The power of aids, and also deeds,
> The vehicle of the intelligent
> Is renowned as the greatest of the great.'

One cognises oneself as having the nature of a very pure deity, and empowering blessings are generated through keeping the pledges of the Conquerors. Also, acting in a way similar to the Conquerors and their sons, one effects the welfare of sentient beings and acts to purify lands. Ratnakarashanti thereby explains that because the objects, aids and concordant deeds are more extensive, the Mantra Vehicle is superior to the Madhyamika of the Perfection Vehicle. It is explained that the Vehicle having these three attributes is divided into the tantra sets of Action, Performance, Yoga and Highest Yoga; thus, these three attributes are asserted to be general features of Mantra.

In short, the view ascertaining that phenomena are empty of inherent existence and the deity yoga of generating oneself as a deity conjointly achieve the fruit, the Two Bodies. This means of achievement is the sole path of passage of all the chief trainees for whom the Vajra Vehicle was set forth. One should know that the many paths other than these two, which are explained in the individual sets of tantras, are either methods for heightening cognition of emptiness or branches of deity yoga. Knowing this, one should hold [these two] to be their essential meaning.

Dispelling Objections

Objection: It is not right to posit inferiority and superiority using the reason that the Perfection Vehicle does not have a cause that accords with a Form Body whereas the Mantra Vehicle does. For it is by no means certain that an effect is always achieved through a cause which accords with that effect. If in order to achieve an effect, which is a body adorned with the major and minor marks, it were necessary as its cause to cultivate a path that has these aspects, then it would be necessary, for instance, to cultivate a path that has them as a cause for achieving a body adorned with the auspicious marks of a Universal Monarch.[62] Furthermore, on all occasions of accumulating the causes for acquiring a body of a happy migration or a bad migration one would have to achieve a cause that has the aspect of those two types of migrators. Both of these consequences are extremely absurd. However, if it is not necessary to have a cause that accords in aspect with these effects, one must find a correct reason why [the opposite] should be applied to Buddhahood, but such cannot be found. Therefore, it is merely an object of faith to state that the achievement of a Form Body by means of a path having the aspect of that Body is a special feature of the Mantra Vehicle.

Answer: I will explain this. Those of the Perfection Vehicle assert that the causes of the entity of a Form Body are the superior collections of merit. The causes of the features which are the major and minor marks and so forth are to provide welcoming and parting escort for a guru and so forth. Through the force of having accumulated these over many lives, a Bodhisattva—when he has arrived at a high ground—attains a body adorned with similitudes of the major and minor marks. These become more and more glorious, and finally during his last lifetime he attains the final major and minor marks of a learner. Then, on this base he actualises a Truth Body, and a similar type of his body having the major and minor marks becomes an Enjoyment Body. Thus, in the Perfection Vehicle they do not assert that on the path there are no major and minor marks, which then arise newly upon attaining the fruit.

In the same way, those of the Vajra Vehicle also do not assert that when Buddhahood is achieved in one lifetime, the final major and minor marks adventitiously arise without there being, when on the path, major and minor marks that accord with those of a non-learner. Therefore, it is the system of both Mahayanas that if on the path of learning the major and minor marks are absent, a Form Body cannot be achieved.

It is not said in Mantra that a beginner engaging in Mantra who will become fully enlightened in his present life must have been born with a body adorned with the major and minor marks; also, such does not exist. Therefore, the major and minor marks of his own body cannot act as the cause of those marks of a Form Body. Through meditation he must newly achieve in this life a cause that is similar in type to the major and minor marks, and this is only possible through deity yoga.

With respect to acquiring a body of a happy or bad migration, it is not necessary to accumulate causes that have such aspects at the time of the causes, but prior to the achievement of a Buddha's Form Body there is a need for causes that accord in aspect with it. How could these two ever be similar? We do not assert that one must cultivate a path that has the aspect of a Form Body for a *cause of maturation* in the sense of taking birth with such a Body. We assert that prior to achieving a Buddha's major and minor marks one needs *causes of similar type* that accord with a Form Body. Therefore, this is not a source of dispute.

Question: In the case of cultivating deity yoga in the three lower sets of tantras and even in Highest Yoga Tantra in cases where Buddhahood is achieved not in this lifetime but over a continuum of lives, how is cultivation of deity yoga a concordant cause of a Form Body?

Answer: Their meditation in this lifetime serves as a cause of similar type when finally they achieve a Form Body in another birth, but it does not cause maturation in the sense of being born with a Form Body.

Having thus eliminated the doubts as they have been set forth, you must gain conviction that cultivation of deity yoga is indispensible. The first chapter of the *Vajradaka Tantra (Vajraḍāka,* a Highest Yoga Tantra) says:

> Oneself is all Buddhas
> And all the Heroes. Through
> Union with one's own deity
> Its nature is thoroughly achieved.
>
> Through this all Buddhas,
> And all the Heroes,
> And all Vajradharas
> Are achieved in this very life.
>
> Vajradakas, Vajrasattvas,
> Tathagatas, and glorious
> Blessed Ones having superior bliss
> In union with all Sky Goers say this.

Also:

> Through this application of a Seal
> He eats all the three grounds [of form].
> If otherwise, the application cannot be
> Complete, and he passes away like a flame.

137

Bhavabhadra's *Commentary on the Vajradaka (Vajra-ḍākavivṛti)*[63] says:

'Through this' refers to the Seal of emptiness [a divine body qualified by emptiness] mentioned just before. This term is used for one who applies in an equal manner [the wisdom of emptiness and the method of deity yoga through] a conventional Seal with hands, face, and so forth. What does this yogi do? 'He eats all the three grounds.' This means that he overcomes ordinary forms such as those of a body. In order to indicate that through mere concentration on emptiness enlightenment will not be achieved, the text says, 'If otherwise, the application cannot be complete, and he passes away like a flame.' 'Otherwise' means 'through only emptiness'. 'The application cannot complete' means that he has passed beyond appearance. 'Passes' means that he passes away from sorrow without even [fulfilling] his own welfare. How? Like a flame. A flame shines and burns into the sky by way of a continuum of oil, but when the oil is exhausted, it too is extinguished and dies. If it does not then illumine itself, what need is there to say anything about its illumining others? One should similarly view meditative stabilisation only on emptiness.

It is the excellent thought of the sets of tantras that if your path of Mantra does not involve cultivating deity yoga, then no matter how much you meditate on emptiness and so forth, when the fruit matures, you cannot avoid falling to an extreme of peace. If you do not gain strong conviction in this, you will forsake deity yoga and practise only a portion of the Mantra path. You should know that this means you have not at all found the corpus of the Mantra path.

One Goal

Though the Paths Have Differences,
Their Fruits Do Not Differ as to Superiority and Inferiority

This section has two parts, the actual meaning and the difference between the Perfection and Mantra paths.

Actual Meaning of the Different Paths'
Not Having Different Fruits

Objection: If the paths of the two vehicles have superiority and inferiority, then so do their objects of attainment—Buddhahood. For, if the causes differ, it would be contradictory if the effects did not; otherwise, the difference in causes would be senseless. Therefore, the eleventh ground of complete light is lower than that of Vajradhara. The fourth chapter of the first division of the *Samputa Tantra* says:

> In brief the Buddhahood
> Achieved over countless
> Or ten million aeons
> You will attain in this birth
> Through the most excellent bliss,
> Or [the ground of] Vajradhara.

This text explains that Buddhahood, which is attained over ten million or countless aeons, and Vajradharahood are different. It also says, 'In this birth you will attain either Buddhahood or Vajrasattvahood. Those who have not attained the inconceivable state are Tathagatas, Buddhas. To illustrate what is to be illustrated [that is, the one who attains the inconceivable state] he is called [Vajra] sattva.'

Answer: [Your interpretation] is not correct. This passage does not teach that through the path of Highest Yoga one achieves in a single life either the ground of complete light which is set forth in the Perfection Vehicle or the ground of Vajradhara which is set forth in Mantra. Also, not even those of the Perfection Vehicle assert that there is no difference between [the tenth Bodhisattva ground called] 'Buddha' which is attained over countless aeons and the eleventh of complete light. For there are two types of attainments over countless aeons; one is a 'Buddha' who is a tenth ground Bodhisattva called a Buddha [whereas the other is an actual Buddha of the eleventh ground]. Maitreya's *Ornament for the Realisations* says:

> Having passed beyond the ninth ground, the wisdom
> By which one abides on the ground of a Buddha
> Is to be known as the tenth
> Ground of a Bodhisattva.

The Vajradhara ground [actual Buddhahood] is the eleventh ground. Though there are explanations in Mantra of twelfth, thirteenth, and fourteenth grounds, Indian scholars have explained them as divisions of those in the Perfection Vehicle. I will explain this later when dealing with the fruit [at the end of the section on Highest Yoga Tantra].

You should know that the eleventh ground of complete light and Vajradhara are the same, that in the sets of sutras it can be achieved over three countless aeons, and in the sets of tantras in one lifetime. You should not hold that because it is called Vajradhara it is not a fruit of the Perfection Vehicle. Shantirakshita's *Text on the Establishment of the Principles (Tattvasiddhināmaprakaraṇa)*[64] says, 'The glorious great bliss, Vajrasattva—the object of realisation by other paths over many countless aeons—is achieved without difficulty in this lifetime itself by those who possess the method of the

Vajra Vehicle.' Thus, the glorious Shantirakshita says that Vajradharahood is the object of attainment for both paths.

Also, Abhayakara's commentary on the passage from the *Samputa Tantra* [p. 139] in his *Clusters of Quintessential Instructions* says, '"Buddha" refers to a lord of the tenth ground. "High Buddha" is the attainment of a special path. "Vajradhara" refers to a lord of the eleventh ground.' Also, Tripitakamala's *Lamp for the Three Modes*[65] says:

> Though the object is the same, mantra treatises
> Are superior because of being for the non-obscured,
> Having many skilful methods, no difficulties, and
> Being contrived for those with sharp faculties.

The objector himself asserts that this means that the object of attainment of the Mantra and Perfection Vehicles is the same.

Furthermore, the Perfection Vehicle explains that one who has attained the ground of complete light has abandoned the two obstructions along with their predisposing latencies and has attained all Buddha attributes such as the powers, fearlessnesses and unshared qualities. If there were something superior to the Buddhahood explained in the Perfection Vehicle, one would have to assert that although the two obstructions were removed along with their predisposing latencies, there would still be defects to remove. One would have to accept that although the hundred and forty-four uncontaminated qualities, such as the ten powers, had been attained, one would still not have completed the auspicious attributes. Therefore, it is suitable to analyse—as many Indian scholars have—whether, without depending on the Mantra path, one can or cannot proceed to such a state using only the paths explained in

141

the Perfection Vehicle; however, it is wrong to assert that one can progress to the ground of complete light by the Perfection path alone but that still one has to progress higher.

The modes of progress on the Perfection and Mantra paths differ as to inferiority and superiority in the sense that on the former one cannot and on the latter one can become fully enlightened without relying on countless aeons [of practice]. However, this does not cause the fruits to differ in quality. This in turn is no proof, however, that the difference in causes is purposeless because, even though the fruits do not differ in quality, they do so greatly in terms of how distant or close they are.

Difference Between the Perfection and Mantra Paths

This section has two parts, the difference according to our own system and the explanations of other masters.

Difference Between the Perfection and Mantra Paths According to Our Own System

The difference in speed between the three lower tantras and the Perfection Vehicle is that [in the paths of the three lower tantras] the practices of enlightenment are completed through many common achievements depending on the powers of deity yoga and repetition, and through many skilful means such as being directly sustained and empowered by Buddhas and great Bodhisattvas. The difference in speed in Highest Yoga Tantra is that even the stage of generation has many profound essentials missing in the lower sets of tantras while the stage of completion has supreme profound essentials. These will be explained later.

A difference in speed due to the development of full enlightenment without relying on the passage of countless aeons is a distinguishing feature of Highest Yoga. Such attainment by the trainees of the lower sets of tantras depends on their entering into the two stages of Highest Yoga; their own paths alone are not sufficient. Thus, it should not be held that all differences of speed in Mantra are only due to the development of full enlightenment in one life in this age of conflict or to the development of full enlightenment without relying on countless aeons [of practice].

Difference Between the Perfection and Mantra Paths According to [Faulty] Explanations of Other Masters

This section has two parts, the difference according to Ratnarakshita's *Commentary on the Difficult Points of the Samvarodaya Tantra (Saṃvarodayapañjikā)* and Tripiti-kamala's *Lamp for the Three Modes.*

Difference Between the Perfection and Mantra Paths according to Ratnarakshita's 'Commentary on the Samvarodaya Tantra'

Ratnarakshita explains[66] that meditation on freedom from elaborations [of inherent existence, conventionalities, and duality] at the stage of completion is similar in both [Mantra and Perfection]. He also points out that the *Meeting of Father and Son Sutra (Pitāputrasamāgama)* says that for a Bodhisattva who has attained the meditative stabilisation of bliss pervading all phenomena, only a feeling of pleasure arises with respect to all objects; pain and neutrality do not occur, and even though [pieces from his body] the size of a small coin (*kārṣhāpaṇa*) are cut or even though his body is crushed by elephants, only a discrimination of bliss is maintained. Ratnarakshita says that this bliss [which is a quality of the Perfection Vehicle] does not conflict with the Mantra Vehicle [mistakenly

143

assuming that this bliss is the same as that in Mantra] and that this sutra even sets forth its method. He says [correctly] that the main cause of all mundane and supramundane marvels is said to be the mind of enlightenment in the Perfection Vehicle and that the same is taught in Mantra. Quoting the *Appearances Shining as Vajras* and so forth as sources, he 'proves' that even great bliss is common [to both the Mantra and Perfection paths].

[Ratnarakshita points out correctly that] Maitreya's *Ornament for the Realisations* says, '[Bodhisattvas of the Perfection Vehicle] are skilled in the means of using desire,' and that the *Kashyapa Chapter Sutra (Kāshyapaparivarta)* says through the example of a farmer that the manure of the afflictions is important for growing Buddha qualities. Thereby [he shows correctly that] engaging in objects of the desire realm is common to both vehicles. Also, [though he correctly explains that] the ground of the fruit and so forth are similar in both vehicles, he [mistakenly] draws the conclusion that the stage of generation is the distinguishing feature of Mantra.

Ratnarakshita says in commentary on the thirteenth chapter of the *Samvarodaya Tantra*,[67] 'Therefore if one does not cultivate the stage of generation, [one's practice] has no feature from the way of Mantra.' He says this [mistakenly] thinking that all cultivations of deity yoga are included in the stage of generation [whereas deity yoga occurs not only in both stages of Highest Yoga Tantra (generation and completion) but also in the three lower tantras], that the yogas of the channels, winds, and drops[68] are for generating bliss [whereas these generate the innate bliss realising emptiness], and that bliss is similar [in both vehicles, whereas there is a great difference].

*Difference Between the Perfection and Mantra Paths
according to Tripitakamala's 'Lamp for the Three Modes'*

Tripitakamala's *Lamp for the Three Modes*[69] says:

> Though the object is the same, mantra treatises
> Are superior because of being for the non-obscured,
> Having many skilful methods, no difficulties and
> Being contrived for those with sharp faculties.

He says that the fruit—omniscience—does not differ in the Mantra and Perfection Vehicles, but that the four sets of tantras are superior to the Perfection Vehicle by way of four features.

Tripitakamala's Faulty Interpretation

Mantra's feature of being for the non-obscured: When those of the Perfection Vehicle engage in giving and so forth, they do so without apprehending [the inherent existence of] the three spheres [of agent, action, and object]; therefore, they are not very obscured. However, since they engage in external giving such as giving away one's head and so forth, they do not have very sharp faculties; thus, they achieve enlightenment over a long period.

Those who train in the Mantra approach do not have this obscuration. For, a perfection is the ability to fulfil a want of all sentient beings simultaneously, and, because giving away one's head and so forth cannot help limitless sentient beings, Mantra practitioners see that a perfection is a fruit of meditative stabilisation. Looking down on ordinary [giving and so forth], they seek a superior method. Through cultivating continuously and without excluding any direction the meditative stabilisation of non-duality of method and wisdom, the welfare of limitless sentient beings can be fulfilled. Thereby the perfection of giving is completed along with the remaining perfections. Because the ordinary giving of a body and so forth does not involve this, it is not posited as a perfection.

145

Mantra's feature of having many methods: The asceticisms, vows, disciplines, and so forth that are set forth in the Perfection Vehicle as methods for high status [within cyclic existence] and liberation [from that existence] accord with training in very peaceful activities; therefore, these cannot take care of all sentient beings. In Mantra four sets of tantras were set forth for the sake of effecting the welfare of all sentient beings. Concerning this, one first realises what type of affliction is predominant in oneself, and then, as in the case of desire, one generates oneself as Amitabha and enters a mind mandala of [mentally] repeating a mantra, a speech mandala of generating the vowels and consonants as deities, and a body mandala of meditating on an immeasurable palace together with its base. Thus, three different approaches are set forth [for one affliction].

Mantra's feature of having no difficulties: Whether or not there is difficulty depends on the mind and not necessarily on any particular phenomenon, because what is difficult for some is easy for others. That which leads a person in accordance with his desires brings about the attainment of bliss through bliss; thus, difficult deeds are not taught in Mantra.

[In Mantra practices are set forth in accordance with trainees' faculties as follows:] The best among those with superior faculties—who are not involved in the faults of desire and so forth, have little discursiveness, but are great in compassion and are striving toward non-dual suchness—are taught the Great Seal [indivisibility of wisdom and method].[70] This is also called 'method and wisdom'—the entity of the wisdom of selflessness being of one taste with great compassion.

The middling [among those with superior] faculties have turned away from enjoying ordinary objects, but have not forsaken thoughts of desire and so forth. They are not able to enter the ocean of ultimate wisdom, and for them meditation on a Wisdom Seal [a meditated consort] is taught. Jnanakirti's *Abridged Explanation of All the Word*[71] explains that they meditate on the five lineages of Tathagatas and their Knowledge Women,[72] the goddesses Lochana and so forth. He explains the way that suchness is entered through meditating on deities: The mind itself, when fixed firmly on a deity's body, appears as the deity and there is no external object. Thereby one comes to understand the teaching not to adhere to the three spheres of an object of meditation, meditating, and meditator. One then abides in a body free from thoughts of external objects and of subject and object. Also, one understands through a guru's quintessential instructions that these bodies do not inherently exist because of being neither one nor many. Then, one understands that all phenomena likewise do not inherently exist. Thinking of this, Buddha set forth limitless deity meditations.

The least among those with superior faculties take joy in non-dual wisdom, but they have not abandoned the desires of the desire realm; through approaching a desirable object their minds are distracted and do not enter into meditative stabilisation. They are allowed Pledge Seals [actual consorts] that possess the attributes of Knowledge Women explained elsewhere [in tantras, such as qualities of form, beauty, age, lineage, excellent training in the mantras and tantras, and maintenance of the tantric pledges].

Action Seals [actual consorts not necessarily endowed with all attributes][73] are taught for those whose desire is very great, whose knowledge of suchness is not great, and whose minds cannot attain equipoise through other methods. Here also they practise by acting in accordance [with divinity by contemplating the consort as having a mantra body of a deity and a nature of wisdom and by contemplating themselves in the form of an omniscient Buddha wrought from great compassion].

With respect to this [last group], Tripitakamala's *Lamp for the Three Modes* does not explain the type of faculty or what Action Seals are but Jnanakirti[74] explains that the least among those with superior faculties have either Pledge or Action Seals. [With regard to the difference between these two] Jnanakirti probably is referring to whether or not these actually engage in the act or whether or not the Knowledge Women are fully qualified.

Therefore, among trainees engaging in Mantra who have the best faculties, those who do not desire the desire realm attributes of a Knowledge Woman [either meditated or actual] are taught meditation on the Great Seal [indivisibility of method and wisdom not involving a consort of any type]. Among those who desire the desire realm attributes of a Knowledge Woman, those who do not desire an external Knowledge Woman [an actual consort] are taught meditation on a Wisdom Seal [a meditated consort]. Those who desire an external Knowledge Woman are permitted both Pledge Seals and Action Seals [fully qualified and not fully qualified actual consorts]. Thus, it would be contradictory to claim this system of the master [Tripitakamala] as one's own and to assert [as is right] that the chief trainees of Highest Yoga must have great desire for the desire realm attributes of an external Knowledge Woman.

Mantra's feature of being contrived for those with sharp faculties: The master Tripitakamala explains that yogis of the four noble truths do not know suchness; therefore, they have dull faculties. Yogis of the perfections are mistaken with respect to method; therefore, they have middling faculties. Those engaging in the Mantra approach are not obscured from anything; therefore, they have sharp faculties because with skill in means they use what would cause others to go to bad migrations and through it they attain a very pure state.

Jnanakirti's *Abridged Explanation of All the Word*[75] says:

> Those who dislike meditation
> On a Wisdom Seal and so forth
> Have little force of wisdom, thus they
> Should not meditate on the Great Seal.
>
> To help them the omniscient one
> Teaches the very forms themselves
> Of Vajrasattva and so forth
> With the name of a Great Seal.

He explains that for those who cannot meditate on the Great Seal due to little strength in wisdom and who dislike meditating on the other three Seals [Wisdom, Pledge, and

Action], a body of a deity is taught with the name of a Great Seal, this being the meditation of the Yoga Tantras. Through this [he says] one can also understand [the meditation of] Performance and Action Tantras.

Refutation of These Positions

Even those of the Perfection Vehicle assert that great compassion—the method—and wisdom cognising suchness—the selflessness of phenomena—are the life of the path. If a perfection of giving involved fulfilling the wishes of sentient beings through giving away material things such as one's head, the perfection of giving would never be completed. This position is refuted by the followers of the Perfection Vehicle themselves, saying that the perfection of giving means to purify the stains of miserliness and of selfish grasping toward all property and to increase the mind of giving to its highest limit. Shantideva's *Engaging in the Bodhisattva Deeds (Bodhisattvacharyāvatāra* V. 9–10) says:

> If through eliminating the poverty
> Of beings, a perfection of giving occurred,
> Then since there are still poor beings, how did
> The former protectors achieve perfection?
>
> Through an attitude of giving to all beings
> All one's possessions with their fruits
> A perfection of giving is said to occur,
> Thus it is just in attitude.

Therefore, Tripitakamala's explanation of Mantra's feature of non-obscuration appears to be in trouble. The feature of being for those with sharp faculties also appears to be in trouble because if it is taken as meaning [its trainees are] not obscured with respect to method, it would be a repetition of the feature of non-obscuration. If it is

149

asserted as using desire for the attributes of the desire realm in the path, then, since the highest trainees of Mantra do not have such desire [according to this wrong interpretation], this feature would be absent in the chief trainees of Mantra.

Also, it is [correctly] explained in many places that the best trainees engaging in Mantra are led completely through the first stage [of generation], then are led on the second stage [of completion], and, when that stage becomes firm, engage in behaviour in dependence on a Knowledge Woman and thereby become fully enlightened in that lifetime. Therefore, this assertion that meditation on a Wisdom Seal and the granting of a Pledge Seal and so forth are for those of middling and low faculties appears to be in trouble. Thus, the discriminative should analyse these and other assertions.

Many Tibetan lamas explain that 'many methods' means many collections of activities of pacification and so forth, and they explain that 'no difficulties' means using the attributes of the desire realm in the path. However, such does not appear in the works of either the master Tripitakamala or Jnanakirti.

Identifying the Four Tantras

*Detailed Explanation of the Forms of Entry
to the Vajra Vehicle*

This section has three parts: number of doors of entry to Mantra, identification of the features establishing the different doors and modes of advancing on the paths possessing these features.

Number of Doors of Entry to Mantra

The thirteenth chapter of the *Vajrapanjara*[76] says:

> Action Tantras are for the inferior.
> Yoga without actions is for those above them.
> The supreme Yoga is for supreme beings.
> The Highest Yoga is for those above them.

With respect to the trainees of the Vajra Vehicle, four sets of tantras were set forth for the lowly, the middling who are above them, the supreme and the very supreme who are above them. Thus, there are four doors of entry from the viewpoint of four sets of tantras.

Also, Shraddhakaravarma's *Introduction to the Meaning of the Highest Yoga Tantras*[77] explains, 'There are four types of approaches for engaging in the Secret Mantra, Effect, Vajra Vehicle. These are generally renowned as Action, Performance, Yoga and Highest Yoga Tantras.'

*Identification of the Features Establishing the
Different Doors of Entry to the Vajra Vehicle*

This section has a question and an answer.

151

Question about the Features Establishing the
Different Doors of Entry to the Vajra Vehicle

The doors of entry to Mantra, which are different grades in the sets of tantras from the viewpoint of lower and higher trainees, cannot be posited by way of lower and higher objects of intent or attainments. For all those who enter the Vajra Vehicle do not differ as to their having generated the Mahayana aspiration, seeking highest enlightenment [as their attainment] for the sake of all sentient beings [their objects of intent]. Also, the differences between the doors of entry to Mantra do not depend on their differing in their general paths that serve as the main causes of the attainment, the Two Bodies. For they are similar in that a Truth Body is achieved through the wisdom cognising non-inherent existence, and they are also generally alike in that a Form Body is achieved through cultivating deity yoga. Hence, they are all the one vehicle called the Vajra Vehicle.

If individual vehicles or doors of entry that are different grades in the sets of tantras could be posited merely through the presence of many different path attributes such as various deity yogas, then there would also have to be many different vehicles in each of the Highest Yoga Tantras. There would also be many doors of entry that would be different sets of tantras even in one Highest Yoga Tantra such as the *Guhyasamaja*, for the *Compendium of Wisdom Vajras (Jñānavajrasamuchchaya*, an explanation of the *Guhyasamaja)* says that there are five types of persons, lower and higher—lotus, sandalwood [white lotus, utpala, and jewel].

Therefore, it should be explained why four doors of entry to Mantra are presented as different sets of tantras from the viewpoint of higher and lower trainees.

Answer

This section has two parts, incorrectness of others' answers and our own answer.

Incorrectness of Others' Answers Regarding the Features Establishing the Different Doors of Entry to the Vajra Vehicle

Some Tibetan lamas[78] say that the four sets of tantras were taught for the sake of accommodating the four lineages among Forders (*Tīrthika*): the desirous who are followers of Ishvara, the hateful who are followers of Vishnu, the ignorant who are followers of Brahma, and the indefinite who hold the tenets of whichever of these they encounter. They are respectively taught Highest Yoga, Performance, Action and Yoga Tantras. Some Tibetan lamas say that Anandagarbha, Rap-jor-kyang [Rab-'byor-bskyangs, Subhūtipālita (?)] and so forth assert this following the *Compendium of Principles*.

However, even if this is interpreted as meaning that there are instances of these types being trained by these tantras, such cannot identify the different features of those who engage in Mantra through the four sets of tantras. This is because some persons of all four types are tamed by each of these tantras.

It would be most unreasonable to assert that such persons are needed as the chief trainees of these sets of tantras. Since the main trainees of the Mantra Vehicle are the superior among trainees engaging in the Conqueror's teaching, they do not have to assume a wrong view before engaging in Mantra. Also, there would be the fault that those who initially engaged in the correct instead of wrong tenets would not be chief trainees of these tantras.

Moreover, this is not the assertion of the master Anandagarbha; the first chapter of his *Commentary on the Guhyasamaja Tantra (Guhyasamājaṭīkā)* says:

Because the Blessed One abides there, 'vagina' indicates the place. The four goddesses called Lochana, Mamaki, Pandaravasini and Tara are here the consorts; they are taught in the seventh chapter of this text. Why does he abide in their secret place? This is for the sake of generating a liking for the abandonment of desire through desire in those who delight in the tantras of Vishnu and the others, and who have not completely abandoned the objects [of desire]. It is this way: They wish to achieve Vishnu and the others through using women, excrement, urine and so forth. Those engaged in seeking feats taught by Vishnu will enter into a consort's secret.

> The blessed vagina is Vishnu
> Abiding in the female genitals.
> Because it gives men pleasure,
> It is called Narayana.

Thus, Anandagarbha states explicitly that those who like the *Vishnu Tantra* are taught through such passages the deeds of desire of Highest Yoga [and, therefore, the interpretation given above could not be his].

There is no way that this presentation that Highest Yoga was taught for these trainees [the desirous who are followers of Ishvara] could come from the *Compendium of Principles*. It appears that these lamas only put this together, drawing [unjustified] conclusions from [the teaching] that four divisions of the *Compendium of Principles* were taught for those who have the afflictions of desire, anger, and so forth. Thus, a valid source [for the theory that the four tantras were taught for four lineages of Forders] is not to be seen.

Also, some Tibetan lamas[79] say that the four sets of tantras were presented from the viewpoint of four different rites of deity generation in accordance with the four schools of tenets. They explain that the Superior Nagarjuna with his sons and Jnanapada with his followers assert the same, following the *Compendium of Wisdom Vajras*. It appears that since these masters are followers of the *Guhyasamaja Tantra*, the lamas are drawing [unjustified] conclusions from the teaching in its explanatory tantra, *Compendium of Wisdom Vajras*, that in Action Tantras there is no pride in oneself as a deity and no bliss of a wisdom being. Thus, no source is seen for a comparison with the four schools of tenets. Even [if one mistakenly imagined] a relation between Solitary Realisers and the rites of generation in Yoga Tantra, Solitary Realisers are not a division of the four schools of tenets [which are Vaibhashika, Sautrantika, Chittamatra and Madhyamika]. Also, I will explain later [in the section on Action Tantra] that the passage in the *Compendium of Wisdom Vajras* does not mean that there is no generation of oneself as a deity in the Action Tantras [but that there are some types of Action Tantra trainees who are frightened and terrified by one-pointed cultivation of deity yoga]. Therefore, this presentation is wrong.

Then, Alamkakalasha asserts [in his *Commentary on the Vajra Garland Tantra (Vajramālāṭīkā)*[80]] that Brahmins are taught Action Tantra and those of the royal caste (*kṣhatriya*) are taught Yoga Tantra. Those in the merchant caste (*vaishya*) whose desire and hatred are slight but whose ignorance is extremely great and who believe in Vishnu are taught Performance Tantra. Those in the merchant caste whose desire and hatred are great but whose ignorance is slight are taught Yoga Tantra such as the *Guhyasamaja* [which is actually a Highest Yoga Tantra]. Those who are related to the servant caste (*shūdra*) whose desire and hatred are the great of the great and whose ignorance is the slight of the slight are taught mother tantras such as the *Little Samvara Tantra (Laghusaṃvara)*.

155

If Alamkakalasha propounds this thinking that there is similarity between the trainees of the four tantras and the four castes, such does not encompass the different features of those who engage in Mantra through the four sets of tantras. If it is asserted that the four castes are needed for the trainees of the four tantra sets, this is not seen to be correct because such is never definite and is not even predominantly so. Though the deities of, for instance, the vajra element [taught in the *Compendium of Principles*] are explained as having features that accord with kings and their retinue, it does not prove that trainees [of Yoga Tantra] are members of the royal caste.

In general, the chief trainees of Mahayana must have strong compassion. In particular, the chief trainees of Highest Yoga wish to attain Buddhahood extremely quickly in order to accomplish the welfare of others due to their being highly moved by great compassion. Therefore, it is nonsense to propound that they must have very great hatred.

Our Own Answer Regarding the Features Establishing the Different Doors of Entry to the Vajra Vehicle

The presentation of four different doors of entry to Mantra by way of tantra sets does not mean that these are different vehicles and is not merely due to there being different features of path such as of deity yoga. Rather, because the main trainees in the Vajra Vehicle are of four very different types, four doors of entry are posited.

The different features of trainees occur in two ways: four different ways of using desire for the attributes of the desire realm in the path and four levels of capacity through which the emptiness and deity yogas that use desire in the path are generated in the mental continuum. With respect to these, the first[81] is set forth in the third chapter of the sixth division of the *Samputa Tantra*:[82]

156

The four aspects of laughing, looking,
Holding hands and the two embracing,
Reside as the four tantras
In the manner of insects.

The *Hevajra Tantra* also makes a similar presentation. Abhayakara's *Clusters of Quintessential Instructions* explains this passage in the *Samputa Tantra* in terms of path tantras but not as tantra texts; however, his *Clusters*, commenting on the first chapter of the seventh division, explains it in terms of tantra texts while Viryavajra explains it in terms of the four sets of tantras in his *Commentary on the Samputa Tantra (Samputaṭīkā)*. The eleventh chapter of the *Ornament of the Vajra Essence Tantra (Vajrahṛdayālaṃkāra)* after setting forth many types of desire tantras within method tantras, says:

> This shows the tantra divisions
> Through the embrace of the two.
> Similarly know them through
> Holding hands, laughing, and looking.

Through speaking in terms of tantras as communicators [texts], the passage indicates the difference between the four sets of tantras. Thus, the sets of tantras are also called tantras of looking [Action], laughing [Performance], holding hands or embracing [Yoga], and union of the two [Highest Yoga].

As was explained before, the special cause of a Form Body is deity yoga, which is the main method. That methods act as heighteners of the wisdom cognising emptiness is the system of both Mahayanas. Shantideva's *Engaging in the Bodhisattva Deeds* [IX.I] says:

> The Subduer said that all these
> Branches are for the sake of wisdom.

157

The way that the path of wisdom is heightened through deity yoga is this: The special method and wisdom is a deity yoga, that is, the appearance of one's chosen deity in the aspect of a father and mother union. Though Highest Yoga has many distinctive features in its path, it is called 'tantra of union of the two' from this point of view, and in these tantras themselves there are a great many descriptions of deities in the aspect of union. From this approach one uses desire in the path and develops the essential of the meeting and staying together of the two minds of enlightenment.[83] In dependence on this, the cognition of emptiness is heightened.

Because the lower tantras lack this special method of using desire in the path, among the seven branches[84] the one of union is not taught in the three lower tantras. Still, because the lower tantras do use joy arising from laughing, looking, and holding hands or embracing in the path, in general they do use desire for the attributes of the desire realm in the path. The twenty-fifth cluster of Abhayakara's *Clusters*[85] says, 'Action, Performance, Yoga and Highest Yoga Tantras are illustrated by way of laughing, looking, embracing or holding hands, and union of the two. Thus, in some Action Tantras and so forth the means by which the desire of the god and goddess—Wisdom and Method—is shown is looking; in some [Performance Tantras], smiling; in some [Yoga Tantras], holding hands; in some [Yoga Tantras], embracing; in some [Highest Yoga Tantras], uniting the two.' Also, the third chapter of the continuation of the *Hevajra Tantra* says:

> Through laughing and looking,
> Embracing and uniting
> The tantras are of four types.

On this Ratnakarashanti's *Commentary on the Difficult Points of the Hevajra Tantra (Hevajrapañjikā)*[86] says,

' "Four" means Action, Performance, Yoga and Highest Yoga Tantras which are illustrated by laughing, looking, embracing and union of the two. Thus, in some Action Tantras and so forth there is smiling that indicates the desire of the god and goddess, Method and Wisdom; in some, after that there is looking; in some, embracing; and in some, union of the two.'

When he says 'The gods look' this means that, as in the case of laughing and so forth, the lookers are the gods. What is the function of looking and so forth? These are the means by which the desires of Wisdom and Method are shown; the god and goddess show desire for each other in these ways. Furthermore, because the deities—Vairochana, Lochana, and so forth—never have desire, here one must apply this to practitioners who take pride in being these deities. For the meaning at this point is that the trainees of the tantra sets should use desire, such as in looking, in the path. Also, if the statements in Action, Performance, Yoga and Highest Yoga Tantras of the male and female deities' looking at each other and so forth are not applied to the trainees, one cannot identify their different trainees from this viewpoint.

Furthermore, not only are laughing and so forth set out in Highest Yoga [as a way of identifying the four tantras], but so are individual instances in the lower sets of tantras. The *Detailed Rite of Amoghapasha (Amoghapāshakalparāja)* [an Action Tantra] says, 'The Blessed One faces Bhrkuti.' Also, 'He aims his eye to the right at the goddess Tara, bashful and with bent body, [displaying] the seal[87] of bestowing the supreme. On the left Sundari of the lotus lineage, bashful, according with the ways of Secret Mantra, aims her eye at Amoghapasha.' The *Vairochanabhisambodhi (Vairochanābhisaṃbodhi)* [a Performance Tantra] says:

> On the right the goddess called
> Buddhalochana, one with
> A slightly smiling face.
> With a circle of light a full fathom,
> Her unequalled body is most clear,
> She is the consort of Shakyamuni.

Also:

> Draw an Ávalokiteshvara,
> Like a conch, a jasmine and a moon,
> Hero, sitting on a white lotus seat.
> On his head sits Amitabha,
> His face is wonderfully smiling.
> On his right is the goddess
> Known as Tara, granting
> Happiness and removing fright.

The *Vajrashekhara* [a Yoga Tantra] says:

> Clasped round the waist, the vajra
> Goddess makes sounds. To his side
> His own goddess turns her head.
> Smiling and looking intently
> She holds the Blessed One's hands.

The *Paramadya (Paramādya)* [a Yoga Tantra] says:

> On that side is Mahavajra
> Holding an arrow upright.
> His proud embracing hand raises
> A banner of victory
> [Adorned] with monsters of the sea.

These are only illustrations [of looking, and so forth]. The practitioner generates himself as the appropriate deity and uses in the path the joyous bliss that arises from their mutual desire, such as in their looking at each other.

In the lower sets of tantras this is not done while observing an external Seal [an actual consort], and even in the higher set of tantras [Highest Yoga] it is not taught that such is done [in the lower tantras]; therefore, these should be understood as meditated goddesses, such as Lochana.

Based on the thought that trainees of little power cannot use great desire in the path, desire is taught for use in the path in stages beginning with small ones. As will be explained, it is clear that when deity yoga has become firm and meditative stabilisation on emptiness has been attained, one takes cognisance of a goddess, such as Lochana, who is of one's own lineage, and then uses [desire in the path by way of looking and so forth]. Viryavajra's *Commentary on the Samputa Tantra* says:

The text says, 'Laughing, looking, holding hands'. This means that within the sound of laughter non-conceptual bliss is generated; or it is generated from looking at the body, the touch of holding hands and the embrace of the two; or from the touch [of union]. 'In the manner of insects' indicates non-contaminated great bliss and emptiness; just as an insect is generated from wood and then eats the wood itself, so meditative stabilisation is generated from bliss [in dependence on desire] and is cultivated as emptiness [whereupon desire is consumed].

The twenty-third chapter of Abhayakara's *Clusters*[88] says, 'A tantra of laughing is, for instance, like the bliss of those of the [divine land called] "Liking Emanation".' Such statements merely cite gods as examples; they do not teach that these gods are the chief trainees of the tantra sets.

Though this is uncertain in terms of *all* who believe in the Vajra Vehicle and those who cultivate some aspects of its paths, the *chief trainees* initially engaging in the Vajra

Vehicle are of the desire realm, and in general they believe in seeking enlightenment through only using in the path desire for the desire realm attributes of a Knowledge Woman. Highest Yoga teaches using the desire of laughing and so forth in the path in cognisance of both actual and meditated Knowledge Women, but in the three lower tantras the joy observing the desire realm attributes of only meditated Wisdom Knowledge Women is used in the path. Since in Yoga Tantras even meditating on a union of the organs is inappropriate, joy that is based on another type of touch—holding hands or embracing—is used in the path. Joy that arises in dependence on observing laughing and looking—but not touching—is used in the path in Performance and Action Tantras. The meanings of the names of the four tantra sets, designated in Highest Yoga [as tantras of looking, laughing, holding hands or embracing, and union of the two], are explained through these distinctions, and thus the differences of their trainees and paths are indicated.

I will now explain the designation of the names of the four tantra sets in accordance with how these names are commonly known in the higher and lower sets of tantras [as Action, Performance, Yoga, and Highest Yoga] and will thereby explain the difference of their trainees. The means of using such attributes of the desire realm in the path are the emptiness and deity yogas. Those who resort to a great many external activities in order to actualise these two yogas are trainees of Action Tantras. Those who balance their external activities and internal meditative stabilisation without using very many activities are trainees of Performance Tantras. Those who mainly rely on meditative stabilisation and resort to only few external activities are trainees of Yoga Tantras. Those who do not rely on external activities and are able to generate the yoga of which there is none higher are trainees of Highest Yoga Tantras.

This explanation of the trainees is done in accordance with the meaning of the names [of the four tantra sets]. For Action Tantras are so called because activities are predominant. Performance Tantras are so called because activities and meditative stabilisation are performed equally. Yoga Tantras are so called because internal yoga is very central. Highest Yoga Tantras are so called because there is no higher yoga.

The names of the four tantra sets are thus explained in accordance with their main trainees who are engaged in the path, but there is no certainty [that all trainees will conform]. For, Anandagarbha explains in his *Illumination of the 'Compendium of Principles'*[89] that the continuation of the continuation of the *Compendium of Principles* was set forth for those who are frightened and scared by cultivation [of deity yoga]. Also, though trainees in general are more, or less, interested in external activities and in cultivation of yoga, there are instances of interest in a path that does not fit a person's faculties; thus, the main trainees of the four tantra sets cannot be identified through interest. Therefore, it should be realised that explanations of their main trainees as relying or not relying on many or few external activities and so forth are correct.

Tripitakamala's *Lamp for the Three Modes*[90] says:

By the force of potencies from conditioning in another birth, some cannot attain mental equipoise without a home in the forest away from people, or without activities such as bathing, drawing mandala, offering, burnt offerings, asceticism, and repetition [of mantra]. Thus, Action Tantras were taught for them. Also, there are those whose minds adhere to suchness and who through the power of faith achieve wisdom by means of activities set forth by the Sugata [One Gone to Bliss, Buddha]. They rely on activities, and for them the

163

Fundamental Tantras that do not have too many branches of activities were set forth.

'Fundamental Tantras' are the same as Performance Tantras.

Tantras are assigned as Action if they predominantly teach external activities even though they contain internal meditative stabilisation. Buddhaguhya's *Word Commentary on the Vairochanabhisambodhi (Vairochanābhisaṃbodhitantrabhāṣhya)*[91] says, 'Action Tantras are mainly concerned with external practices, but internal practices are not absent.' Also, Vajragarbha's *Commentary on the Condensation of the Hevajra Tantra (Hevajrapiṇḍārthaṭīkā)* explains that [tantras spoken for] those who have little capacity for meditation on suchness[92] but are mainly involved in external activities are Action Tantras.

Tantras are assigned as Performance if they teach internal meditative stabilisation and external activities equally. Buddhaguhya's *Word Commentary on the Vairochanabhisambodhi*[93] says, 'Although this tantra is a Performance Tantra mainly involving method and wisdom, it also teaches practice of activities in order to accommodate migrators who are trainees inclined toward activities. Therefore, it is designated and known as an Action Tantra or a Both Tantra [Performance Tantra].' The *Ornament of the Vajra Essence Tantra* also makes reference to 'Both Tantra', saying, 'Action, Both, and Yoga Tantras'.

Tripitakamala's *Lamp for the Three Modes*[94] says, 'Others are interested solely in meditation on non-dual suchness and mainly engage in yoga because they consider groups of many activities to be distracting. For them Performance Tantras that secondarily teach only a few branches of activities were set forth.' Here, 'Performance Tantras' means Yoga Tantras.

Preparation for Mantra

Modes of Advancing on the Paths
Possessing These Features

This section has two parts: common stages of the path in the two Mahayanas and uncommon ones in the Vajra Vehicle. [Only the first part is translated here.]

Common Stages of the Path in the Two Mahayanas

The *Vajrapani Initiation Tantra (Vajrapāṇyabhiṣheka)* says:

'This very vast, very profound mandala of the great retention mantras[95] of the great Bodhisattvas, difficult to penetrate, more secret than the secret, which is not fit to be shown to sinful sentient beings, has been mentioned very rarely by you, O Vajrapani. How can it be explained to sentient beings who have not heard it before?'

Vajrapani said, 'Manjushri, those Bodhisattvas who practise the Bodhisattva deeds through the approach of Secret Mantra, when they have engaged in and achieved cultivation of the altruistic mind of enlightenment, may enter the mandala of retention mantras where the initiation for great wisdom is bestowed. Those who have not completely achieved this are not to enter; they should not even be allowed to see a mandala; they should not be shown seals [hand symbols] or secret mantras.

Thus, it is said that prior to bestowing initiation the altruistic mind of enlightenment must be completed.

165

Therefore, first you should train in the aspirational and practical minds of enlightenment and then enter a mandala.

The stages of training in the aspirational and practical minds of enlightenment are these: Initially you should rely in the proper way on a qualified spiritual guide of the Mahayana through thought and deed. He will teach the ways in which leisure is meaningful and difficult to find, and, through training the mind in this, a great wish to extract the essence of this life-support of leisure will be generated. The best means to do so is to enter the Mahayana. The door of entry to the Mahayana is just the altruistic mind of enlightenment because, if it actually exists in your mental continuum, your being a Mahayanist is not artificial, whereas if it is only verbal, your being a Mahayanist is also only verbal. Therefore, an intelligent person should gradually remove whatever is discordant with the altruistic mind of enlightenment and generate it with all its characteristics.

If you do not initially turn your mind away from this life, it is an obstacle to the paths of either Hinayana or Mahayana. You should be mindful of death in the sense that you will not stay long in this life and should think how after death you may wander to bad migrations; you should thereby turn your mind away from this life. Then, your attachment to the marvels of a future life should be overcome through good thinking about the faults of all cyclic existence; thereby, your mind will be inclined toward liberation.

After that, to overcome the attitude of seeking the bliss of peace for yourself, you should train for a long time in love, compassion and the altruistic mind of enlighten-ment—which has love and compassion as its root—and then practise a non-artificial mind of enlightenment. Next, you should come to know the Bodhisattva deeds and generate a wish to train in them. If you can bear the burden of the deeds of Conqueror Sons, you should take the Bodhisattva vows and practise its precepts. Then, if you can take on the burden of the pledges and vows of the Vajra Vehicle, you should listen to Ashvaghosha's *Fifty Stanzas on the Guru (Gurupañchāshikā)* and, having purified the modes of reliance on a guru, enter into Mantra.

The *Fifty Stanzas on the Guru* says:

> To a student with pure thought who has
> Gone for refuge to the Three Jewels
> This [text on] following a guru
> Should be given for recitation.
> Then through giving him mantra[96] and so forth
> He is made a vessel of excellent doctrine.

The *Fifty Stanzas on the Guru* is to be explained to one who has trained in 'pure thought'—the altruistic mind of enlightenment—and who has taken the uncommon refuge. After the master gives the *Fifty Stanzas on the Guru*, [the recipient] is made into a vessel [of Mantra] through initiation.

Rahulashrimitra's *Clarification of Union (Yuganaddhaprakāsha)*[97] says:

> The stages are these: at a time of joy
> By the date, constellations and so forth,
> The student with pressed palms and bending down
> Should confess all his sins
> And take the three refuges.
> He should practise well the mind
> Of enlightenment and take
> The lay and Bodhisattva vows
> And purification and renewal.
> In concordant stages he should rely
> In excellent ways on a Vajra master,

But fearing here to take too long
I will write no more about it.
Having done all this he should ask his guru,
'Please bestow initiation on me.'

Prior to initiation one should take [a vow of] individual emancipation, generate an altruistic mind of enlightenment and its vow, and then petition a guru for the bestowal of initiation. The lay vow and its purification [of infractions against vows previously taken] and renewal [restoring sullied vows to purity] refer to a householder; a monk who is entering into Mantra should keep in all purity the vows of a novice and so forth.

The first chapter of Aryadeva's *Lamp Compendium of Practice*[98] after proving that one should train in stages and not in everything at once, says, 'The stages are these: First one trains in the thought of the Buddha Vehicle. When one has done so, one trains in a new vehicle, the meditative stabilisation of single mindfulness.' After one has previously trained in the Buddha Vehicle—its thought being the aspirational and practical minds of enlightenment—one trains in a new vehicle—Mantra.

Therefore, the need to generate the aspirational and practical minds of enlightenment and to be endowed with the deeds of the six perfections is not merely carried over here from the Perfection Vehicle, for the Mantra texts themselves say again and again that one should train in these paths. These are common paths appearing in the Vajra Vehicle itself. Since I have explained them extensively in *Stages of the Path Common to the Vehicles*, I will not elaborate here.

Not discriminating with stainless reasoning
The difference between good and bad explanations
In our own and others' systems, and without
Discriminating correctly the main features
Common and uncommon in Hinayana, Mahayana,

Mantra and Perfection, it is only an act of
    faith
To propound that the general Buddhist teaching,
Mahayana, and especially the Vajra Vehicle
Are the supreme doors of entry for the
    fortunate.
Thus, O, O, you with intelligence and aspiration,
Until you cannot be stirred by a challenger
Train the eye of intellect with right
    reasoning
And seek firm conviction in the teaching's
    essentials.

The first section of *Revealing All Secret Topics, The Stages of the Path to a Great Vajradhara*, called 'General Teaching of the Doors of Different Stages for Entry to the Teaching', is concluded.

169

III
Supplement

JEFFREY HOPKINS

Emptiness

Tsong-ka-pa says that only the Buddhist teaching is the entrance of those wishing liberation from cyclic existence and that within Buddhism it is only through understanding the Prasangika-Madhyamika presentation of emptiness that the ability to eradicate suffering can be gained.[99] Emptiness as explained by the Prasangikas is considered to be more subtle than that expounded by any other system. Other systems are helps and aids and, though a particular person might progress more now by assuming one of them rather than attempting to penetrate Prasangika, the subtle emptiness must eventually be understood. All practices lead to the centre by creating the capacity to practise the one path that actually arrives at the centre. The actual final arrival is on only one path.

Though a Hinayana path is not final, for a Hinayanist it is a means to highest enlightenment, Buddhahood. In this context, 'Hinayana' and 'Mahayana' refer not to the four Buddhist schools of tenets, two Hinayana—Vaibhashika and Sautrantika—and two Mahayana—Chittamatra and Madhyamika—but to the Hinayana and Mahayana *paths* that each of the four schools presents. (See chart 1.) Hinayana paths are for people bearing the lineage of Hearers and Solitary Realisers, and Mahayana paths are for those bearing the lineage of Bodhisattvas. Among the four presentations of Hinayana and Mahayana paths, Tsong-ka-pa here clarifies the presentation of the final system, Prasangika-Madhyamika.

'Mahayana' sometimes refers to the Chittamatra and Madhyamika schools of tenets and at other times refers to the Bodhisattva path, as presented by either Hinayana or Mahayana schools of tenets, for even the Hinayana

173

CHART 1: FOUR SCHOOLS AND THREE VEHICLES

School	vehicle	effect

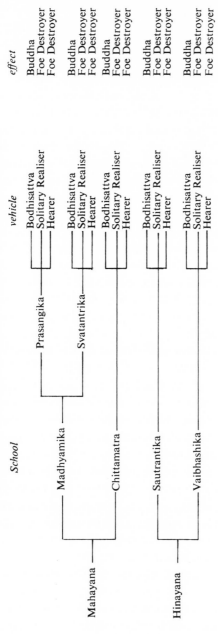

School — Madhyamika — Prasangika
— Svatantrika
— Chittamatra

Hinayana — Sautrantika
— Vaibhashika

vehicle (for each):
Bodhisattva
Solitary Realiser
Hearer

effect (for each):
Buddha
Foe Destroyer
Foe Destroyer

schools propound a Bodhisattva path. Vaibhashika and Sautrantika—the Hinayana schools—accept the rendition of Buddha as a Bodhisattva in his *Birth Tales (Jātaka)* and in the discipline (*vinaya*) division of the scriptures. According to the Hinayana schools Shakyamuni Buddha is the only one to complete the Bodhisattva path in our era.

According to Vaibhashika and Sautrantika, Hearer and Solitary Realiser Foe Destroyers (*Arhan*) are lower than a Buddha. All three are equally liberated from cyclic existence and will all equally disappear upon death with the severance of their continuum of consciousness and form. However, while they are alive, a Bodhisattva at the effect stage is called a Buddha whereas the others are only called Foe Destroyers—those who have destroyed the foe of the afflictions, mainly desire, hatred, and ignorance—because a Buddha has special knowledge, more subtle clairvoyance, and a distinctive body. A Bodhisattva accumulates merit and wisdom for three countless aeons, thus attaining the greater fruit of Buddhahood. For Vaibhashika and Sautrantika, a person treading the path of Buddhahood is very rare.

Both Hinayana tenet systems present three vehicles which they say are capable of bearing practitioners to their desired fruit. Both present an emptiness that must be understood in order to reach the goal, and in both systems this emptiness is the non-substantiality of persons. They prove that a person is not a self-sufficient entity and does not substantially exist as the controller of mind and body, like a lord over his subjects. Through realising and becoming accustomed to this insubstantiality, the afflictions and, thereby, all sufferings are said to be destroyed. According to the Hinayana tenet systems the path of wisdom is the same for Hinayanists—Hearers and Solitary Realisers—and for Bodhisattvas. The length of time that practitioners spend amassing meritorious power constitutes the essential difference between the vehicles.

175

The Mahayana systems—Chittamatra and Madhyamika, the latter being further divided into Svatantrika and Prasangika—do not just describe or report the Vaibhashika and Sautrantika assertions on Hinayana but present their own Hinayana paths. For instance, according to the Prasangika system, one must understand the subtle emptiness—non-inherent existence—of persons and other phenomena in order to leave cyclic existence. Therefore, Hearers and Solitary Realisers must understand the subtle emptiness just as Bodhisattvas do. According to Prasangika, the difference between the Hinayana path of Hearers and Solitary Realisers and the Mahayana path of Bodhisattvas is that Mahayanists have succeeded in generating an altruistic aspiration to highest enlightenment for the sake of all sentient beings which is induced by love and compassion. When this altruistic aspiration arises spontaneously—whether going, wandering, lying, or sitting just as strongly as it does in meditation—then one is a Bodhisattva and a Mahayanist by path, not just by tenet.

A Prasangika by tenet would certainly want to generate love, compassion, and the altruistic aspiration, but in the meantime he might have developed to the point of spontaneity merely the wish to leave cyclic existence. In that case, he would be a Hinayanist by path, though a Mahayanist by tenet. In other words, when he has practised over a long time to the point where the thought of renunciation arises spontaneously night and day—whether going, wandering, lying, or sitting, never for a moment admiring the prosperity of cyclic existence—then he achieves the bottom line of the Hinayana path, the path of accumulation. He might temporarily lay aside full development of altruism, seeking instead to relieve only his own pressed situation. As a Prasangika, he would concentrate on the emptiness of inherent existence rather than the coarser emptiness of substantial existence as presented in Vaibhashika and Sautrantika. This Hinayana way is said to be a more protracted path to Buddhahood than immediately extending one's understanding of the plight of cyclic existence to others, developing love and compassion, and engaging in meditation on emptiness in order to achieve others' welfare by becoming a Buddha.

According to Prasangika, the basis of a Bodhisattva's practice is generation of an altruistic aspiration to highest enlightenment for the sake of all sentient beings. A Bodhisattva engages in the six perfections—giving, ethics, patience, effort, concentration, and wisdom—in limitless varieties for at least three countless aeons in order to empower his mind so that he may overcome the obstructions to omniscience. He attains liberation from cyclic existence at the beginning of the eighth of the ten Bodhisattva grounds after two countless aeons of practice, spending this vast length of time amassing meritorious power in order to empower his mind to counteract the appearance of objects as if they cover their own parts, or bases of designation.

The teaching that such a tremendous length of time is required to destroy these obstructions inspires a yogi to develop a willingness for long-term practice; he imagines practically limitless future lives involving practice of the six perfections. A Bodhisattva becomes like a mother holding her baby who kicks her, pulls her hair, and sticks a finger in her eye. She is patient, knowing how long her task will take. In the same way, a Bodhisattva is willing to spend an aeon to achieve one slight improvement in one sentient being.

Though a Bodhisattva must practise for two countless aeons before he attains liberation from cyclic existence whereas a Hearer can leave cyclic existence in as little as three lifetimes, a Bodhisattva has engaged in the meantime in a path that will make his eventual attainment of Buddhahood much faster. (See chart 2.) When a Hearer devotes time to his own welfare, he pollutes his mind with

CHART 2: PATHS

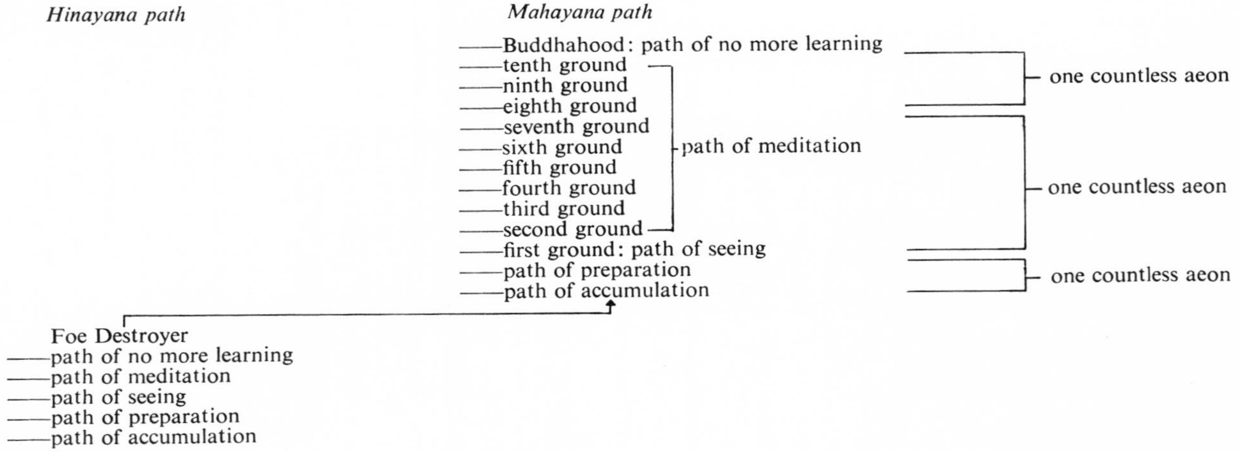

Hinayana path

Mahayana path

Buddhahood: path of no more learning
tenth ground
ninth ground
eighth ground
seventh ground
sixth ground
fifth ground
fourth ground — path of meditation
third ground
second ground
first ground: path of seeing
path of preparation
path of accumulation

one countless aeon

one countless aeon

one countless aeon

Foe Destroyer
path of no more learning
path of meditation
path of seeing
path of preparation
path of accumulation

self-cherishing such that it lengthens the path to Buddhahood. Still, Hearers and Solitary Realisers all eventually proceed to the Bodhisattva path. After sometimes spending aeons in solitary trance, they are aroused by Buddhas who make them aware that they have not fulfilled even their own welfare, not to mention the welfare of others, and they finally enter the Bodhisattva vehicle. Thus, though there are three vehicles, there is only one final vehicle.

According to the Prasangika system, Hearers and Solitary Realisers have the most subtle wisdom, cognising the subtle selflessness of both persons and phenomena, whereas, according to the Chittamatra and Svatantrika systems, Hearers and Solitary Realisers do not cognise the subtle selflessness of phenomena and thus do not have the most subtle wisdom. Vaibhashika, Sautrantika, Chittamatra, and Svatantrika all assert that Hearers and Solitary Realisers are liberated from cyclic existence through cognising and accustoming to merely the subtle selflessness of the person. Let us examine this.

Selflessness is divided into two types: of persons and of phenomena. The selflessness of persons is also divided into two: coarse and subtle. (See chart 3.) Vaibhashika and Sautrantika do not assert a selflessness of phenomena because, for them, phenomena truly exist and are other entities from a perceiving consciousness.

With regard to the personal selflessness, all systems present subtle and coarse forms. According to the non-Prasangika systems the coarse is the emptiness of a permanent, partless, independent person. The misconception of such a self is only artificial, not innate—it is based only on the assumption of a non-Buddhist system. In other words, we do not naturally misconceive the person to have the three qualities of permanence, partlessness, and independence.

According to all systems except Prasangika, the subtle

179

CHART 3: SELFLESSNESS

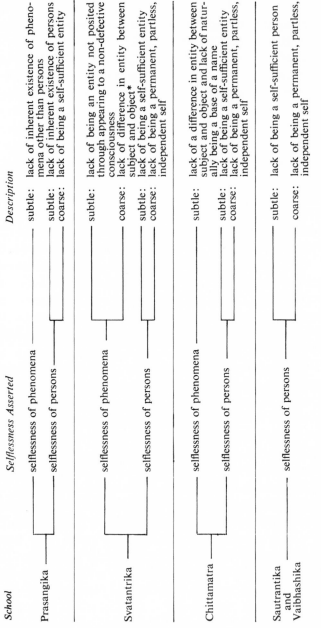

School	Selflessness Asserted	Description
Prasangika	selflessness of phenomena	subtle: lack of inherent existence of phenomena other than persons
	selflessness of persons	subtle: lack of inherent existence of persons coarse: lack of being a self-sufficient entity
Svatantrika	selflessness of phenomena	subtle: lack of being an entity not posited through appearing to a non-defective consciousness coarse: lack of difference in entity between subject and object*
	selflessness of persons	subtle: lack of being a self-sufficient entity coarse: lack of being a permanent, partless, independent self
Chittamatra	selflessness of phenomena	subtle: lack of a difference in entity between subject and object and lack of naturally being a base of a name
	selflessness of persons	subtle: lack of being a self-sufficient entity coarse: lack of being a permanent, partless, independent self
Sautrantika and Vaibhashika	selflessness of persons	subtle: lack of being a self-sufficient person coarse: lack of being a permanent, partless, independent self

*asserted only by Yogachara-Svatantrika

personal selflessness is the emptiness of a self-sufficient or substantially existent person. Here a yogi cognises that a person does not substantially exist or exist as a self-sufficient entity in the sense of being the controller of mind and body. The mind and body falsely seem to depend on the person whereas the person does not seem to depend on mind and body. The person seems like a master, and mind and body his subjects; this misconception is of two types, artificial and innate, the former being a conception of substantial existence reinforced by a system of thought and the latter being an habitual or untutored conception. Most religions, philosophies, and systems of psychology reinforce these innate misconceptions, thereby compounding the basic error with further superimposition.

The Chittamatra system asserts the subtle selflessness of persons in the same way as Vaibhashika and Sautrantika but they also assert a selflessness of phenomena that is more profound and subtle; it is an emptiness of a difference in entity between subject and object. Subject and object—apprehender and apprehended—appear to be distant and cut off but are not so in reality. A yogi attempts through reasoning and examples, such as similarity with dreams, to overcome assent to this false appearance and finally to remove the mistaken aspect in all appearance.

In Madhyamika, the selflessness of phenomena is the emptiness of a mode of subsistence not posited by the mind. Things seem to have their own independent existence—their own mode of existence without being posited through appearing to the mind—whereas they are actually posited only through appearing to the mind, much as a magician's illusion is posited to be real through appearing to the audience's spell-bound mind. The Prasangika sub-division of Madhyamika further refines this selflessness as an emptiness of inherent existence, which means that objects are not even the collection of their parts and are only designated to that collection.

181

Though phenomena appear to exist concretely, when sought analytically they are unfindable. As in the Chittamatra system, yogis meditate in order to overcome assent to this false appearance of concreteness and eventually to empower the mind such that the mistaken element disappears entirely.

In the non-Prasangika systems, Hearers and Solitary Realisers only cognise the selflessness of persons. These systems say that a person falsely seems to have a character different from the character of mind and body which they exemplify with a master and his subjects, the former controlling the latter. The Prasangikas, as presented by Jam-yang-shay-ba, a late seventeenth and early eighteenth century Gelukpa scholar, say that mind and body seem to be like salesmen and the person like a head salesman. The difference is that a head salesman is a salesman, but a master is not a servant. The person falsely seems to be the boss, seems to be in control of mind and body, but not necessarily as a separate entity. Thus, according to the Prasangika system, there is no *innate* conception of a self of persons—coarse or subtle—in which the person is conceived to be a different entity from mind and body.

What the non-Prasangika systems identify as the subtle selflessness of persons, the Prasangikas identify as the coarse selflessness of persons, and further what the non-Prasangikas describe as the innate subtle conception of a self of persons, the Prasangikas identify as artificial and coarse. This means that according to Prasangika we conceive the person to have a different character or different entity from mind and body only based on mistaken philosophies. Therefore, according to this highest of systems, we cannot leave cyclic existence through cognising the selflessness of the person as described by the other systems. Not only that, but also the other systems have not accurately delineated what is refuted in the coarse personal selflessness.

According to Chittamatra and Svatantrika, Bodhisattvas are more intelligent than Hearers and Solitary Realisers and thus perceive a deeper, more fundamental emptiness—the selflessness of phenomena—thereby eradicating a more basic problem. Prasangika, on the other hand, considers what others describe as the subtle selflessness of persons as the coarse selflessness of persons; the others' subtle selflessness is then replaced by the emptiness of an inherently existent person. Prasangika also substitutes inherent existence for difference of entity between subject and object. Thus, in this system, that which is negated in the theory of emptiness is the same in both the selflessness of persons and the selflessness of phenomena—inherent existence in both cases. Here, there is no difference in depth or subtlety between the selflessness of persons and of phenomena.

The Chittamatrins assert that the lack of difference in entity between subject and object is the subtle selflessness of phenomena. The Svatantrikas say that the lack of existence which is not posited through the object's appearing to the mind is the subtle selflessness of phenomena, and in both Chittamatra and Svatantrika the subtle selflessness of phenomena is subtler than the subtle selflessness of persons. One has to be brighter, sharper, to understand it, and Bodhisattvas are sharper. However, when Prasangikas assign the non-inherent existence of persons as the subtle personal selflessness and the non-inherent existence of other phenomena as the subtle selflessness of phenomena, there is no difference in subtlety between the two. Once the one had been cognised, the other could be cognised.

Consequently, according to Prasangika—the final system in Tibet—it is impossible to be liberated from cyclic existence without understanding the emptiness both of persons and of other phenomena. In this system, both Hearers and Solitary Realisers cognise a selflessness that is subtler than what other systems call subtle; the great Hinayana Foe Destroyers of the past cognised this deepest of emptinesses, and Bodhisattvas do not cognise another more profound reality even though they are brighter. They merely approach this same emptiness through more avenues of reasoning.

Prasangika is the only Mahayana system to assert that one type of realisation is common to all three vehicles. The two Hinayana systems, Vaibhashika and Sautrantika, assert that all three vehicles cognise the same subtle selflessness but this is only the person's non-existence as a self-sufficient or substantially existent entity. Chittamatra and Svatantrika assert that Bodhisattvas realise a deeper emptiness, the selflessness of phenomena, than do Hearers and Solitary Realisers, who realise only the subtle selflessness of persons. Furthermore, among the two divisions of Svatantrika, Yogachara-Svatantrika and Sautrantika-Svatantrika, the former asserts a coarse selflessness of phenomena which is the same as the Chittamatrins' subtle selflessness of phenomena—the lack of a difference in entity between subject and object. As Madhyamikas, they also assert a subtle selflessness of phenomena which is an emptiness of true existence—existence not posited through the object's appearing to the mind. They say that Solitary Realisers meditate on the coarse selflessness of phenomena—non-difference in entity between subject and object; Bodhisattvas meditate on the subtle selflessness of phenomena—non-true existence of all phenomena; and Hearers meditate on the subtle selflessness of persons—non-existence as a substantially existent or self-sufficient entity. Thus, in Yogachara-Svatantrika there are three types of realisation.

The Svatantrikas say that each object has its own particular mode of subsistence but not one that is not posited through the object's appearing to the mind. For example, when a magician creates an attractive feast, it has a mode of subsistence posited by the audience's mistaken mind. The power of a mantra has affected everyone's consciousness, including the magician's. The audience assumes a feast covers that spot in its own independent right, whereas, even though it appears that way to the magician, he does not believe it. He knows its nature and does not posit to it an independent entity. In the same way, phenomena appear to the non-mistaken consciousnesses of sentient beings—eye, ear, nose, tongue, body and mental consciousnesses—and through appearing to the mind, their own particular mode of subsistence is posited, the error being that objects are granted a mode of subsistence independent of appearing to the mind. That which is negated in the view of selflessness is an independent entity of objects.

For the Prasangikas, if something has its own particular mode of subsistence, it is not posited by the mind; the two are contradictory. The Prasangikas assert that everything—be it a person or any other phenomenon—is like a magician's illusion in that it appears to exist inherently but does not. They present a deeper and more subtle object of negation than the other systems, which are considered in Tibet to be ways of overcoming coarser misconceptions. The reason for Buddha's propounding the other non-final systems is said to be that people who would be discouraged by not being able to penetrate the deeper teaching are taught a selflessness that is not so deep but are told that it is the deepest.

The coarse sense of self is easier to identify. For instance, when we are told, 'Your hair is very shiny today,' there is a sense of an 'I' that controls or owns the hair. Or, sometimes when we are accused or praised, there is something very tight and firm, undeniable, unmistakable, almost touchable, seeable, in the centre of the chest—the 'I' who has been offended, hurt, praised, or helped. Sometimes when we examine this 'I' with a subtle

185

non-interfering consciousness while it is operating, it even seems as if it is a different entity. Sometimes, it is more like a lord and his subjects than a head salesman and his salesmen. This is the artificial, coarse conception of a self of persons, and we might progress more from concentrating on it than proceeding to the innate coarse form.

It takes a truly practical and humble devotee of any religion to decide that he cannot succeed at the most subtle teaching at present. To help avoid this problem, even nowadays teachers pretend that they are presenting the view of non-inherent existence but instead present the view of non-substantial existence. Thus, it is not difficult to imagine that Buddha would present another system and say that it is the final system.

This provisionality necessitates a division of the Buddhist scriptures into two classes, definitive and requiring interpretation. The distinction between these is based on whether the main object of discourse is emptiness. If it is, then the mode of existence of the phenomena discussed in that sutra is definite as just what is said in the sutra and does not require interpretation. Scriptures that do not explicitly present emptiness as the main object of discourse require interpretation to know the final mode of existence of the phenomena discussed in those sutras. For instance, Buddha said that there are five aggregates: forms, feelings, discriminations, compositional factors, and consciousnesses. This teaching is literal, definite, and reliable because the existence of the aggregates is certified by valid cognition; however, the teaching requires interpretation to know the final mode of existence of the aggregates—their emptiness of inherent existence.

Within scriptures requiring interpretation, there are two types, literal—as in the example of the aggregates above—and non-literal. Non-literal teachings are not supported by valid cognition and must be interpreted in terms of a particular trainee's need for such a doctrine. For instance, Buddha taught that liberation can be achieved through cognising and accustoming to the four noble truths: true sufferings, true origins, true cessations, and true paths. There are sixteen attributes of the four truths, which in brief are:

true sufferings
1 impermanence
2 misery
3 emptiness
4 selflessness
true origins
1 cause
2 origin
3 strong production
4 condition
true cessations
1 cessation
2 pacification
3 auspiciousness
4 definite emergence
true paths
1 path
2 knowledge
3 achievement
4 deliverance

All Buddhist systems, therefore, hold that true sufferings, the internal and external phenomena of cyclic existence, are impermanent, miserable, empty, and selfless.

Products are impermanent in that they require no further cause for their disintegration than their own production; products have a nature of disintegration. This does not imply chaos, for just as a flame can be steady in a

187

breezeless room, so, if calm abiding (*shamatha*) is developed, the mind can remain steadily fixed on whatever object is chosen. The flame of one moment, however, is not the flame of the next moment.

True sufferings are miserable in that they are involved in actual physical and mental pain itself or, if they are pleasurable, can easily turn into pain. They are empty in the sense that they are not a permanent, partless, independent person or the objects of use of such a person. They are selfless in that they are not a substantially existent person or the objects of use of such a person. Dharmakirti said that knowing emptiness and selflessness is the aim of the other aspects and that these two aspects are the paths of liberation from cyclic existence.

According to the Prasangika system, however, these are merely coarse paths, serving only to train the mind, not to liberate it. Such realisations cannot serve as antidotes to the innate conception that persons naturally or inherently exist. They will lead to liberation but will not liberate.

Therefore, according to Prasangika, Hinayana paths, as presented by Svatantrika, Chittamatra, Sautrantika, and Vaibhashika, are suited for the majority of Hearers and Solitary Realisers, who are for the present incapable of practising a path of liberation and need aids to develop that ability. Because the subsidiary trainees of Hinayana are greater in number than the special trainees, systems particularly suited for them are needed. When the progression of the systems is understood, the variety of approaches not only is not contradictory but is most appropriate, inducing conviction in Buddha's extraordinary ability to teach.

Transformation

Religion requires analysis but not partisanship. In order to penetrate reality, a yogi needs a sharp mind; it dulls the mind to claim that religions are one in all respects, suggesting that the differences in trainees and in practices are of no consequence. Claiming that all religions are one suggests that practice is ineffective.

Tsong-ka-pa's statement that only Buddha taught the final path of liberation draws us into analysis to determine whether or not this path is actually the only final way. A positive decision would indeed impel great effort; an issue of great importance, affecting not just this short lifetime but also the many lifetimes in the future, is at stake. Tsong-ka-pa issues a call to analysis to see if the Buddhist path is true.

The process of passing from a mistaken notion to clear apprehension of the truth is said to pass through seven steps (reading from bottom to top):[100]

7 direct perception
6 inferential cognition
5 correct assumption
4 doubt tending to the factual
3 equal doubt
2 doubt tending to the non-factual
1 wrong view

We begin with a wrong view such as: Buddha, his teaching, and those properly training in his teaching are not the teacher of liberation, the path to liberation, and the friends on the journey to liberation; or, another example: I definitely inherently exist.

Through contact with Buddhist teaching, the wrong view may change into doubt tending to the non-factual: Buddha, his teaching, and those properly training in his path are *probably* not the teacher, path, and friends on the journey to liberation; or: I *probably* inherently exist. Doubt has been raised; the firmness of the wrong view is gone. It is a time of inquiry, leading to equal doubt: Maybe Buddha is the teacher of liberation and maybe he is not; or: Maybe I inherently exist and maybe I do not.

On the basis of study, contact with spiritual guides, and personal experience, doubt tending to the factual is generated: Buddha probably is the teacher of liberation; or: I probably do not inherently exist. Through familiarisation with the logical proofs for omniscience and the efficacy of the path as well as with scripture, correct assumption is generated: Buddha is the teacher of the path to liberation, his teaching is the path, and those properly training in it are the friends on the journey to liberation; or: I do not inherently exist.

Still, assumption is not incontrovertible; though a decision has been made, it has not been induced by incontrovertible conviction. Therefore, a correct assumption about the Three Jewels—Buddha, his Doctrine, and the Spiritual Community—is not sufficient; the unshakable knowledge of inference is needed.

Inference is incontrovertible understanding based on reasoning: Buddha, his teaching, and those properly training in his path have qualities such as omniscience, complete cessation of the afflictions, and ability to aid in the path that can be verified through reasoning. Similarly, it can be proved that the 'I' does not inherently exist through realising that whatever is a dependent-arising does not inherently exist and that the 'I' is a dependent-arising. After repeated inquiry, unshakable conviction is generated; through familiarisation this can be brought to the point of direct cognition, such as directly knowing the true cessation of a certain portion of the afflictions based on Buddha's path or directly knowing emptiness—the non-inherent existence—of the 'I'.

The process of passing from wrong views to the incontrovertible knowledge of cognition, be it inferential or direct, depends on study, analysis, meditation, and acquaintance with a spiritual guide. Inferential understanding is not a discursive mulling over of ideas and concepts; it is the conclusion of the process of analysis in a definite realisation. In the case of emptiness, an image of a mere vacuity appears to a mind that ascertains a negative of inherent existence. This realisation is called inferential and conceptual only because the *image* of a mere vacuity of inherent existence appears, rather than the mere vacuity itself. The mind is stilled; it has understood that the 'I' is a dependent-arising and that whatever is a dependent-arising does not inherently exist; now, it *knows* that the 'I' does not inherently exist. The impact of even attaining a correct assumption about the emptiness of 'I' which means its unfindability among its bases of designation—mind and body—is said to be like being struck by lightning. Thus, inferential cognition, far from being a vague shuffling of concepts, is even more dramatic.

When the ascertainment of non-inherent existence lessens, a yogi reviews the process of reasoning, but otherwise he remains in the *result* of reasoning—in terms of appearance, a mere vacuity of inherent existence and in terms of ascertainment, the definite knowledge of an absence of inherent existence. By stabilising on this mere vacuity and occasionally heightening the realisation by further analysis, a yogi brings this conceptual or imagistic understanding to the point of direct cognition. The sense of the object—emptiness—and the subject—the wisdom consciousness—gradually disappear, leaving a fusion of object and subject, like fresh water poured into fresh water.

191

The resultant cognition is non-dual but not non-specific. As much as colours and shapes can be known definitely and directly by the eye consciousness, so the mental consciousness can know emptiness definitely and directly. The absence of inherent existence is known directly, based on earlier familiarisation with a reasoning proving emptiness. Thus, far from turning against the process of reasoning, this practice is built on reasoning. However, those who are addicted to discursive thought cannot pass to the conclusion of reasoning, much like seeing smoke, reflecting that wherever there is smoke there is fire, and repeatedly going through this process without ever concluding that fire is present.

As much as one can incontrovertibly know of the presence of fire when billows of smoke are seen and can act on that knowledge, so much can one penetrate the nature of phenomena through a similar process of reasoning and live in accordance with it. Also, just as one can eventually go outside and see the fire directly, so by accustoming to the space-like meditative equipoise, one can perceive emptiness directly, without the medium of a mental image.

Although an emptiness is a mere negative of inherent existence, it is amenable to reflection and can eventually be perceived non-conceptually. The *Kashyapa Chapter Sutra* says, 'Kashyapa, it is this way: For example, fire arises when the wind rubs two branches together. Once the fire has arisen, the two branches are burned. Just so, Kashyapa, if you have the correct analytical intellect, a Superior's faculty of wisdom is generated. Through its generation, the correct analytical intellect is consumed.' Right thought overcomes wrong thought and leads to direct knowledge; thus, discrimination based on correct reasoning is the primary means, when coupled with a mind of calm abiding, for developing direct insight. Even the non-conceptual sense consciousnesses have a factor of discrimination, which is a non-confusion of the objects perceived; without it, everything would be a confused mass. This faculty must be developed, first conceptually and then non-conceptually, with respect to the nature of phenomena. Thought must be used to develop indirect knowledge of the nature of phenomena, and, through familiarisation, this is gradually transformed into direct knowledge. Just as the eye consciousness can have definite and certainly not contentless knowledge of a colour, so the mental consciousness can know impermanence, suffering, emptiness, others' minds, and so forth without the medium of concepts or images.

Objection: This progression suggests that there is something new to be known. Nagarjuna said that there is not the slightest difference between cyclic existence (*saṃsāra*) and nirvana.

Answer: The altruistic aspiration to highest enlightenment for the sake of all sentient beings is the basis of a Bodhisattva's practice in both the Perfection Vehicle and the Vajra Vehicle. The altruistic aspiration is induced by love and compassion, which are the result of seeing the suffering of cyclic existence, generating a wish to leave it, and then applying this understanding to others. If one does not want to be free of cyclic existence, there is no way to wish for others to be free of it. This wish to leave cyclic existence is common to Hinayana and Mahayana and within Mahayana is common to the Perfection and Vajra Vehicles.

The Sanskrit word *nirvāṇa* was translated into Tibetan as 'passed beyond sorrow', with 'sorrow' identified as the afflictions, the chief of which is the conception of inherent existence. Cyclic existence is an uncontrolled process of birth, aging, sickness, and death motivated by the afflictions. It is clear that when Nagarjuna says that cyclic

193

existence is nirvana, he is not asserting that cyclic existence is the state of having passed beyond sorrow. Rather, in this context 'cyclic existence' or *saṃsāra* refers to conventional truths, all objects except emptinesses; the term 'nirvana' refers to a natural nirvana, not the nirvana that is the true cessation of all suffering. A natural nirvana does not come into existence in dependence on the path but is merely the emptiness of inherent existence that each object naturally has.

An emptiness is not created by realising it; a yogi realises what always was. 'Natural nirvana' (*svabhāvanirvāṇa*) may also be translated as 'inherent nirvana' though, of course, 'inherent' here does not mean 'inherently existent'. The commentarial tradition in Tibet makes the point that a natural nirvana is not an actual nirvana because an actual nirvana is a true cessation of all afflictions.[101]

Thus, the statement that *saṃsāra* is not in the least different from *nirvāṇa* does not mean that the uncontrolled process of cyclic existence which forms the basis for suffering is the cessation of all suffering. Rather, it refers to the relationship between conventional truths and ultimate truths.

The meaning of Nagarjuna's statement is that there is not the slightest difference in *entity* between a conventional truth, a *saṃsāra*, and its emptiness, a natural *nirvāṇa*. They are different within the context of being included in one entity.

Since conventional truths—all objects except emptinesses—are not ultimate truths—emptinesses—the two truths are not merely two ways of looking at the same object, and thus it cannot be said that a conventional truth, such as a table or a body, and its emptiness, its lack of inherent existence, are one. They are also not synonyms; an ultimate truth is not a conventional truth and a conventional truth is not an ultimate truth. Further, the two truths are a dichotomy because if something exists and is not an ultimate truth it must be a conventional truth, and if something exists and is not an ultimate truth it must be a conventional truth; a dichotomy includes all existents, and nothing can be both.

If a phenomenon, such as a body, and its emptiness were exactly the same, then when we saw the body, we would see its emptiness, in which case we would be liberated. However, we are not liberated; we habitually conceive the opposite of emptiness and are thereby drawn into afflictions. Therefore, ultimate truths and conventional truths are not exactly the same, but they are also not different entities because when one understands the emptiness of the body, for instance, this helps to overcome the misconception of the inherent existence of the body. In other words, because an emptiness of inherent existence is the nature of the body, cognising it helps to overcome misconception of the body. If an emptiness were one entity and the body another, thorough cognition of emptiness would not affect the misconception of phenomena as inherently existent. A conventional truth, such as a body, and an ultimate truth, its emptiness of objective or inherent existence, are compatible in one entity but are different.

Ultimate truths do not contradict conventional truths; the emptiness of the body does not contradict the conventionally and validly existent body; it contradicts its inherent existence. Therefore, 'conventional' does not mean 'usual', because all phenomena usually appear to the non-conceptual sense consciousnesses as if they cover their parts, as if they exist in and of themselves whereas they do not. We know conventional truths such as houses, bodies, and minds, but we do not know conventional truths *as* conventional truths. To know this, we must know emptiness, the non-inherent existence of objects; then, we can understand that objects only nominally exist.

Except for emptinesses, all objects are conventional

truths, or 'truths for an obscured mind'. They seem to exist the way they appear only to a mind obscured with ignorance. Every object has a natural nirvana that is its non-existence in the way it appears, its emptiness of inherent existence. When this is thoroughly known, the afflictions are gradually overcome to the point where all afflictions whatsoever are removed forever. There is then a nirvana, an emptiness of the mind in the continuum of one who has overcome all afflictions.

In order to effect this transformation a yogi cultivates a mind that is a similitude of a Buddha's Truth Body. Using a reasoning analysing the ultimate, he investigates whether mind, body, or 'I' exist as they appear—exist right with their bases of designation, which for mind are moments of consciousness, for body are limbs and a trunk, and for 'I' are mind and body. Intently searching to discover whether the appearance of inherent existence can bear analysis, the yogi gradually discovers that it cannot; a vacuity which is a negative of inherent existence appears with which he fuses his mind, remaining in this space-like meditative equipoise as long as possible. This is the path of wisdom of the Perfection Vehicle, a path of transformation through cultivating prior to the effect stage a similitude of the non-dual meditative equipoise that a Buddha never leaves.

The Vajra Vehicle has the further feature of cultivating while still on the path a similitude of a Buddha's Form Body. These similitudes of Buddha Bodies are cultivated in order to transmute not only the mind but also the process of physical appearance. The goal is still the Buddhahood that serves as the basis for the welfare of all sentient beings, but the method for eradicating desire, hatred, and ignorance involves using these in the path within the context of emptiness and deity yogas. As the Sakya master, Sö-nam-tse-mo (bSod-nams-rtse-mo, 1142–1182) says in his *General Presentation of the Tantra Sets*:[102]

196

If one has method, [desirable] objects serve as aids to liberation, like poison [used as medicine], fire [used in moxabustion], and so forth. Therefore, objects are not inherently fetters; perverse thoughts based on them act as fetters. Through abandoning the entities of the fettering causes, one is liberated; thus, objects serve as secondary causes of liberation. The *Hevajra Tantra* says:

> One is liberated from the fetters
> Of cyclic existence through those that bind,
> When they are accompanied by method.

With respect to the phrase 'accompanied by method', what is the method for abandoning the causes of being bound? . . . Knowing whatever objects and subjects appear as just one's own deity, one enjoys them. The *Guhyasamaja Tantra* says:

> Use as you wish all
> Desired resources,
> With the yoga of your deity
> Offer them to yourself and others.

The Nyingma master Long-chen-rap-jam (kLong-chen-rab-'byams, 1308–1363) says in his *Treasury of Tenets*:[103]

Question: If the Mantra Vehicle partakes of a path purifying defilements, what does it mean that it takes the effect as the path? Since the Cause Vehicle is generated to purify defilements, it would be similar.

Answer: Though the Definition [Perfection] Vehicle and the Mantra Vehicle are the same in simultaneously cleansing the defilements of the realm and achieving Buddhahood, there is a difference of temporal proximity and distance. Also, the mere warmth of the

197

path for which the Definition Vehicle strives over a long time is taken as the path in one instant of Mantra. Furthermore, due to cultivating in meditation a similitude of the state in the mandala of the expanse, even objects of abandonment shine as aids. In this way the effect is taken as the path; however, the exact final fruit is not actually taken as the path. Therefore, it is necessary to cultivate the profound and the vast in meditation.

Mere withdrawal of the mind from conceptions of inherent existence or even mere deity yoga without the wisdom of emptiness will not serve as an antidote to the afflictions. The supreme method is cultivation of deity yoga within the context of realising emptiness of inherent existence. The wisdom consciousness understanding emptiness and fused with emptiness appears as a deity, and within this state what formerly bound one in cyclic existence can be used as aids to liberation.

Deity yoga requires creative imagination; a yogi recognises that his present perceptions are coloured by predispositions established by former actions and in order to gain control over the process of appearance enters into the practice of making ideal substitutions. Through imaginatively causing everything that appears to be conjoined with emptiness and deity yoga, he cleanses innate predispositions for misperception and misconception. However, the distinction between imagination and fact is still made, and Buddhahood has not become a figment of imagination. Long-chen-rap-jam says:[104]

When one has become a Buddha, freed of all defilements, the features of a land appear thoroughly adorned within the context of neither composition nor separation of body and wisdom [which are indivisibly fused]. Such is actualised [in Mantra] through the force of clearing away the defilements that exist in the expanse by meditating on a similitude of such a land. Therefore, it is called the Effect Vehicle. The *Padmashekara Tantra* says:

> When the nature of the stainless expanse
> Having the Three Bodies, wisdom, and land
> Is purified, it manifestly appears
> In self-illumination. This which takes
> A similitude as the path is rightly
> Called the Vehicle of the Effect.

In Mantra, knowledge of the nature that abides primordially in the excellent inherent effect of the expanse is taken as the basis and practised. Therefore, it is called the Effect Vehicle. Furthermore, in terms of clearing away defilements, generation and completion are cultivated, and through training in suchness the adventitious defilements are purified. The gods, mandalas, and so forth which are mentally meditated are fabrications of one's own mind; thus, this is not meditation that takes the effect—the expanse with gods and mandalas—as the actual path. However, because it is close to the meaning of the expanse, it should be viewed as a profound, undeceiving path. Though the Mantra Vehicle is similar to the Cause Vehicle in not being able to take the expanse as the actual path, there is a great difference in the closeness of the paths [to the fruit] due to the difference of having a similarity of feature [with the fruit].

Due to its similarity with the effect and its speed in generating the effect, the Vajra Vehicle is called the Effect Vehicle. The process of transforming body and mind is modelled on the features of the effect being sought. Whereas the Perfection Vehicle has cultivation of only a similitude of a Truth Body and relies on other causes to develop a Form Body, the Vajra Vehicle has cultivation of similitudes of both Bodies. This is its distinguishing and elevating feature, the very life of which is to identify wrong conceptions about the nature of phenomena and gradually discover the meaning of emptiness. For it is the consciousness cognising emptiness that itself appears as the body of a deity.

Purpose of the Four Tantras

Tantras are divided into four sets, Action, Performance, Yoga, and Highest Yoga, by way of trainees' varying abilities to use desire in the path. When desire arising from looking, laughing, holding hands or embracing, and union is used in the path in conjunction with emptiness and deity yogas, desire itself is extinguished. The First Panchen Lama, Lo-sang-chö-ki-gyel-tsen (bLo-bzang-chos-kyi-rgyal-mtshan, 1569–1662), says:[105]

A wood-engendered insect is born from wood but consumes it completely. In the same way, a great bliss is generated in dependence on a causal motivation which is the desire of looking, laughing, holding hands or embracing, or union of the two organs. The wisdom of undifferentiable bliss and emptiness—which is this great bliss generated undifferentiably with a mind cognising emptiness at that same time—consumes completely the afflictions, desire, ignorance, and so forth.

The four tantras are divided on the basis of their main trainees' ability to use in the path these four forms of desire, which correspond to the four types of satisfaction found in the various levels of the desire realm. The gods of the Land of the Thirty-Three and all beings below them, including humans, gain satisfaction through sexual union. The gods of the Land Without Combat gain satisfaction through embracing; those of the Joyous Land, through holding hands; those of the Land of Liking Emanation, through laughing; and those of the Land of Controlling Others' Emanations, through looking. Abhayakara, in

201

explaining the four tantras, uses these gods as *examples*, and Tsong-ka-pa emphasises that Abhayakara does not mean that gods are the main trainees for whom the four tantras were spoken. Four sets of tantras were expounded to accommodate the abilities of four types of persons to use desire in the path.

Alamkakalasha, however, taught that the four tantras were expounded to accommodate the four castes. He explains:[106]

Action Tantras were taught in order to accommodate Brahmins since they like bathing and cleanliness, hold the view that one is liberated through asceticism, consider their caste to be important, and hold that one is liberated through repetition and burnt offerings . . . Performance Tantras, teaching both internal yoga of wisdom and method and external activities, were set forth in order to accommodate the merchant caste since they cannot engage in severe asceticism, will not become involved in low actions, and look down on external cleanliness and so forth. . . . Yoga Tantras [in which the gods and goddesses of the mandalas correspond to a king and his retinue] were taught in order to accommodate those of the royal caste since they cannot engage in asceticism but enjoy the pleasures of the five attributes of the desire realm. . . . Highest Yoga Tantras, which teach the non-conceptual usage of the five fleshes and so forth, as well as low actions, were taught for those of the servant class who without any sense of cleanliness eat everything, engage in all actions, and have little conceptuality.

Tsong-ka-pa points out flaws in this interpretation, which are further elaborated by the First Panchen Lama:[107]

It is wrong to posit the four sets of tantras from the viewpoint of the four castes. If this means that those of the four castes are the special trainees of the four tantras, then this entails the fault of being too broad [since not all members of the castes practice tantra]. If this means that members of the four castes are needed for the main trainees of the four tantras, then this entails the fault of being too narrow [because the main trainees of the four tantras come from any part of society, not from a specific caste]. If this means that there are cases of the four tantras taming members of the four castes, then this entails the fault of indefiniteness [since there are cases of all four taming members of all four; therefore, this could not serve to distinguish the tantras].

Tsong-ka-pa emphasises that it is not even predominantly the case that the trainees of particular tantras would come from a particular part of society. He ridicules the idea that just because Yoga Tantras use mandalas modelled on the royal court, their chief trainees must be members of the royal caste.

It seems more likely that this teaching applying the four tantras to the four castes arose from the usage of caste members as examples. For instance, a master might exhort his initiates that in order to meditate on themselves as the main figure in a Yoga Tantra mandala, they would have to consider themselves as kings; or, in order to practise the strict cleanliness that accompanies certain rituals of Action Tantra, they would have to be like Brahmins, who are famous for bathing many times a day; or, in order to practise the non-differentiation of thoughts of cleanliness and uncleanliness in Highest Yoga Tantra, they would have to be like members of the lowest class.

Another interpretation of the four tantras, reported by both Sö-nam-tse-mo and Bu-tön (Bu-ston, 1290–1364) is that four rites of deity generation were taught to accommodate persons following the four schools of tenets. The tradition is:[108]

1 Just as Vatsiputriyas and Aparantaka-Vaibhashikas assert truly existent external objects and an inexpressible self, so the rite of deity generation in Action Tantras involves laying out a painting of a deity in front of oneself, arranging offerings, bathing, observing cleanliness, inviting a wisdom being [an actual deity] in front of oneself—corresponding to an external object—placing the mantra in his heart, and engaging in repetition within the context of viewing the deity as like a master and oneself as a servant. Just as these schools assert an inexpressible self, so the wisdom being is neither the painting nor oneself.

This interpretation of Action Tantra is based on the teaching in the *Compendium of Wisdom Vajras*, a Highest Yoga Tantra, that in Action Tantras there is neither pride in oneself as a deity nor entry of a wisdom being into oneself (imagining oneself as a deity and then causing the actual deity, the wisdom being, to enter). However, Tsong-ka-pa explains in his exposition of Action Tantra that this passage refers only to the lowest trainees of Action Tantras, who are frightened by meditating on themselves as a deity, not the main trainees of Action Tantra who are fully capable of practising deity yoga.

2 Performance Tantras involving generation of oneself as a symbolic being and generation of a deity in front as a wisdom being were taught for Kashmiri Vaibhashikas and Sautrantikas. Repetition is performed within the context of viewing the deity—the wisdom being in front—and oneself—the symbolic being [imagined as a deity]—as companions. This is similar to these schools' assertion of ultimately existent subject and object.

This apparent similarity is unfounded because the Tantra Vehicle is part of Mahayana from the viewpoints both of tenet and of path. Since emptiness yoga is an integral part of deity generation, adherents to Hinayana tenets are not the main trainees of any tantra, nor does any tantric system propound the ultimate existence of subject and object, the opposite of emptiness.

3 Yoga Tantras involving generation of oneself as a symbolic being and then causing the wisdom being to enter oneself were taught for Solitary Realisers. This rite of deity generation is similar to Solitary Realisers' assertion of conventionally existent object and subject.

This interpretation of Yoga Tantra is based on the Yogachara-Svatantrikas' assertion that Solitary Realisers cognise the non-truth of objects—the non-difference in entity between subject and object. However, 'Solitary Realiser' is not a school of tenets but a type of practitioner whose path is presented by all four schools of tenets, Vaibhashika, Sautrantika, Chittamatra, and Madhyamika.

4 Highest Yoga Tantras were taught for the Mahayana Chittamatrins and Madhyamikas who assert that neither subject nor object ultimately exists but exists only conventionally. These tantras involve generation of oneself as a symbolic being and the entry of a wisdom being—corresponding to asserting subject and object conventionally—but do not involve requesting the deity to leave—corresponding to not asserting either subject or object ultimately.

Again, the similarity is slight and suggests that in the past a master merely indicated differences in rites of deity generation through comparison with differences between schools of tenets, and this was wrongly taken to mean that the tantras were taught for people adhering to those schools of tenets.

Bu-tön, after reporting this tradition, says, 'Tibetan lamas have said this, but I have not seen a source for it.' The Kagyu master Pad-ma-kar-po (Pad-ma-dkar-po, 1527–92) says:[109]

> Some Tibetan teachers have explained that [the tantras] are differentiated into four types based on accommodations to [four types of] Forders or based on four schools of Buddhist tenets. Since the sources that they cite do not appear in any texts, these explanations are only their own thoughts.

The Sakya master Sö-nam-tse-mo reports that this tradition *claimed* to be following Nagarjuna, and as the Geluk master, the First Panchen Lama, says,[110] 'It is not correct that such was asserted by Nagarjuna and Jnanapada because such a presentation was not set forth in any of the writings of these two.'

Because tantra involves the usage of desire, hatred, and ignorance in the path in order to overcome the afflictions and because practices are geared for persons having one or the other affliction predominant, many have assumed that the four tantras were taught for four types of persons dominated by different afflictions. Though a certain affliction in a tantric practitioner may be predominant in the sense of being stronger than the other afflictions, a tantrist is not dominated by afflictions; rather, he has come under the influence of great compassion and is seeking the quickest means of attaining a state where he can effectively help suffering sentient beings. In his *Explanation of the Rite of the Guhyasamaja Mandala*, the Seventh Dalai Lama says with regard to trainees of Highest Yoga Tantra:[111]

Some see that if one relies on the Perfection Vehicle and so forth, one must amass the collections [of merit and wisdom] for three countless great aeons, and thus it would take a long time and involve great difficulty. They cannot bear such hardship and seek to attain Buddhahood in a short time and by a path with little difficulty. These people who claim that they, therefore, are engaging in the short path of the Secret Mantra Vehicle are outside the realm of Mantra trainees. For to be called a Mahayanist in general one cannot seek peace for oneself alone but from the viewpoint of holding others more dear than oneself must be able, for the sake of the welfare of others, to bear whatever type of hardship or suffering might arise. Since Secret Mantrikas are those of extremely sharp faculties within Mahayanists, persons who have turned their backs on others' welfare and want little difficulty for themselves are not even close to the quarter of Highest Secret Mantra. . . . One should engage in Highest Yoga Tantra, the secret short path, with the motivation of altruistic mind generation, unable to bear that sentient beings will be troubled for a long time by cyclic existence in general and by strong sufferings in particular and thinking, 'How nice it would be if I could achieve right now a means to free them!'

As Jang-kya (lCang-skya, 1717–86) says in his *Presentation of Tenets*:[112]

It is said in the precious tantras and in many commentaries that even those trainees of the Mantra Vehicle who have low faculties must have far greater compassion, sharper faculties, and a superior lot than the trainees of sharpest faculties in the Perfection Vehicle. Therefore, those who think and propound that the Mantra Vehicle was taught for persons discouraged

207

about achieving enlightenment over a long time and
with great difficulty make clear that they have no
penetration of the meaning of tantra. Furthermore, the
statement that the Mantra Vehicle is quicker than the
Perfection Vehicle is in relation to trainees who are
suitable vessels, not in terms of just anyone. Therefore,
it is not sufficient that the doctrine be the Mantra
Vehicle; the person must be properly engaged in the
Mantra Vehicle.

Far from being taught for those unable to proceed on the
Perfection Vehicle, the four tantras were expounded for
persons of particularly great compassion who possess
differing abilities to use what usually are causes of cyclic
existence as means to transcend it.

Unfounded traditions on tantra have been widely
reported in the West whereas in Tibet the many traditions
on the reasons for the four tantras were winnowed by
scholar-yogis to derive their own final position. The First
Panchen Lama says:[113]

Our own system is that the reason for positing four
different doors of entry [to the practice of Mantra] from
the viewpoint of four tantras is that the main trainees for
whom the Vajra Vehicle was intended are of four types.
These four types are posited because there are four ways
of using desire for the attributes of the desire realm in
the path and four types of higher and lower capacities
for enhancing the yoga that is a union of the wisdom
cognising emptiness and deity yoga which utilise these
four modes in the path.

The Panchen Lama mentions another misconception of
tantra that is also widely renowned in the West:[114] 'Those
of the Perfection Vehicle cognise the nature of phenomena
by way of examples and reasons whereas here [in the

Mantra Vehicle] emptiness is cognised directly . . .'
Also,[115] 'Those of the Perfection Vehicle believe and
think, "All phenomena are free of conceptual
elaborations", but do not cognise them in this way. Here
[in the Mantra Vehicle] emptiness is cognised directly
through many methods . . .' However, non-dualistic
wisdom is the life of both the sutra and tantra paths, and in
both paths initial reliance on reasoning to uncover the
nature of phenomena, hidden to our direct experience, is
necessary. Through repeated cultivation, conceptual
knowledge of suchness becomes non-conceptual wisdom.
Those who do not view the great texts that set forth the path
of reasoning of the middle way, such as Nagarjuna's
Treatise on the Middle Way, as precepts for practice
mistakenly hold tantra to be merely a different technique
for cognising emptiness. Having discarded the path for
realising emptiness, they—through misapprehending the
meaning of tantra—also discard the special tantric method
for developing the Form Body of a Buddha, deity yoga.

Quintessential Points on the Difference between Hinayana and Mahayana and The Two Mahayanas*

1 The Dalai Lama teaches that one needs to combine learnedness, practical application, and a good mind. Therefore, mere learnedness about the difference between the vehicles is not sufficient.

2 Generation of a good mind is the essential purpose of differentiating the vehicles; the immediate purpose is to know the difference between the vehicles in order to facilitate practice.

Hinayana and Mahayana

3 One can distinguish the terms 'Hinayana' and 'Mahayana' from the viewpoint of schools of tenets and from the viewpoint of path.

4 One can be a Mahayanist by tenet and a Hinayanist by path, as in the case of the great Foe Destroyers of the past. Thus, there are some who are capable of assuming a Mahayana tenet system who are temporarily incapable of generating a Mahayana path.

5 The two Hinayana tenet systems (Vaibhashika and Sautrantika) and the two Mahayana tenet systems (Chittamatra and Madhyamika) each present a Hinayana path (Hearer and Solitary Realiser paths) and a Mahayana path (Bodhisattva path).

*Several points are drawn from the Dalai Lama's *The Buddhism of Tibet and The Key to the Middle Way.*

210

6 The reason for four schools of tenets is persons' differing capacities, including the pride of wanting the highest despite being incapable of it; thus, low, non-final systems are taught as if they were final.

7 The difference between Hinayana and Mahayana and between the two Mahayanas must be found in the sense of vehicle as that to which one progresses (the fruit) and/or as that by which one progresses (method, wisdom, or both).

8 Valid foundation and the conditionable nature of the mind make limitless development of method and wisdom possible.

9 The difference between Hinayana and Mahayana lies in the sense of vehicle as that to which one is progressing (Foe Destroyer and Buddha which bear, like a vehicle, the welfare respectively of only oneself and of all sentient beings) and as those practices by which one progresses (specifically method, not wisdom).

10 From the viewpoint of Prasangika-Madhyamika, the wisdom of both vehicles is the same because the root of cyclic existence is the conception of persons and other phenomena as inherently existent, and Foe Destroyers (those who have attained the fruit of Hinayana paths) are liberated from cyclic existence, having destroyed the foe of afflictive ignorance.

11 Therefore, both Hinayana and Mahayana paths involve realisation of the subtle emptiness which is the lack of inherent existence in persons and other phenomena.

12 Therefore, the difference between Hinayana and Mahayana in the sense of vehicle as that by which one progresses lies not in wisdom but in method—motivation and its attendant deeds. The Hinayana motivation is the wish to attain liberation from cyclic existence for oneself whereas the

211

Mahayana motivation is the wish to attain Buddhahood in order to help all sentient beings.

13 There are two kinds of obstructions: afflictive obstructions (preventing liberation from cyclic existence) and obstructions to omniscience (preventing simultaneous cognition of the two truths—ultimate truths and conventional truths, or emptinesses and the objects qualified by emptiness).

14 The afflictive obstructions are (1) the ignorance conceiving the inherent existence of persons and other phenomena, (2) the other afflictions which this induces, and (3) their seeds.

15 Obstructions to omniscience are predispositions which are established by the *conception* of inherent existence but which produce the false *appearance* of inherent existence as well as the incapacity to cognise the two truths directly and simultaneously.

16 If one's aim is merely to abandon the afflictive obstructions, it is sufficient to approach emptiness through merely a few forms of reasoning. If one's aim is to eradicate the obstructions to omniscience and thereby attain Buddhahood, it is necessary to approach emptiness through limitless forms of reasoning.

17 Thus, although there is no difference in the *type* of wisdom between Hinayana and Mahayana, there is a difference in the mode of cultivation and the eventual effect.

Perfection Vehicle and Mantra Vehicle

18 The two Mahayanas, Perfection Vehicle and Mantra Vehicle, have the same fruit and the same wisdom; therefore, the difference lies in method, which is tantra's special feature of deity yoga.

19 A practitioner of tantra must have particularly

intense compassion, being in great haste to become a Buddha in order to help others.

20 Method in the Perfection and Mantra Vehicles is the same with respect to the basis of practice, which is the altruistic mind of enlightenment, and the deeds of practice, which are the six perfections. Therefore, the Mantra Vehicle does not discard or transcend the conventional mind of enlightenment (the altruistic aspiration to Buddhahood for the sake of others and the Bodhisattva deeds) or the ultimate mind of enlightenment (direct realisation of emptiness by a Bodhisattva). However, Mantra has the additional feature of deity yoga.

21 The difference in speed between the two Mahayanas is due to a faster accumulation of merit in the Mantra Vehicle (if one is capable of practising it), resulting from the cultivation of deity yoga. This involves meditation cultivating a similitude of a Buddha's Form Body, residence, resources, and activities.

22 Emptiness yoga is a general feature of Buddhist deity yoga, distinguishing it from non-Buddhist deity yoga.

23 In emptiness yoga one must confidently stabilise on the vacuity which is a negative of inherent existence found after searching for the concretely existent self which so palpably appears to us.

24 Deity yoga involves causing the mind realising emptiness and fused with that emptiness to itself appear as a deity, out of compassion, in order to help others.

25 'Vajra' means an indivisible union of the wisdom realising emptiness and compassion.

26 The Perfection Vehicle does not have deity yoga even though it has meditation cultivating a similitude of the Truth Body, the space-like meditative equipoise on emptiness.

27 All tantric practices are either deity yoga, emptiness yoga, or enhancers of these two.

28 The Perfection Vehicle *alone* is not sufficient for the attainment of Buddhahood, nor are the three lower tantras *alone*. Highest Yoga Tantra is required for overcoming the extremely subtle obstructions to omniscience.

29 For tantra in general, the difference in speed over the Perfection Vehicle is the passage from the beginning of the path of accumulation to the path of seeing faster than the one period of countless aeons required in the Perfection Vehicle.

30 The attainment of Buddhahood in one lifetime is a distinctive feature of Highest Yoga Tantra. Thus, the greater speed of Mantra over the Perfection Vehicle is not necessarily the attainment of Buddhahood in one lifetime of the degenerate era.

31 Because the practices of the Perfection Vehicle are indispensible to and the very substance of the Mantra Vehicle, we should view even its ancillary practices, such as that of impermanence which is conducive to realising emptiness, as substantial contributors to the Mantra path.

Appendix, Glossary, Bibliography, and Notes

Appendix

An illustration in tabular form of the structure of
Tsong-ka-pa's *Great Exposition of Secret Mantra*

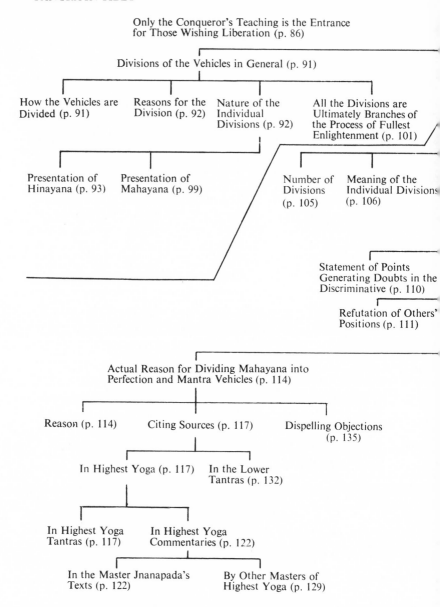

Only the Conqueror's Teaching is the Entrance for Those Wishing Liberation (p. 86)

Divisions of the Vehicles in General (p. 91)

How the Vehicles are Divided (p. 91)

Reasons for the Division (p. 92)

Nature of the Individual Divisions (p. 92)

All the Divisions are Ultimately Branches of the Process of Fullest Enlightenment (p. 101)

Presentation of Hinayana (p. 93)

Presentation of Mahayana (p. 99)

Number of Divisions (p. 105)

Meaning of the Individual Divisions (p. 106)

Statement of Points Generating Doubts in the Discriminative (p. 110)

Refutation of Others' Positions (p. 111)

Actual Reason for Dividing Mahayana into Perfection and Mantra Vehicles (p. 114)

Reason (p. 114)

Citing Sources (p. 117)

Dispelling Objections (p. 135)

In Highest Yoga (p. 117)

In the Lower Tantras (p. 132)

In Highest Yoga Tantras (p. 117)

In Highest Yoga Commentaries (p. 122)

In the Master Jnanapada's Texts (p. 122)

By Other Masters of Highest Yoga (p. 129)

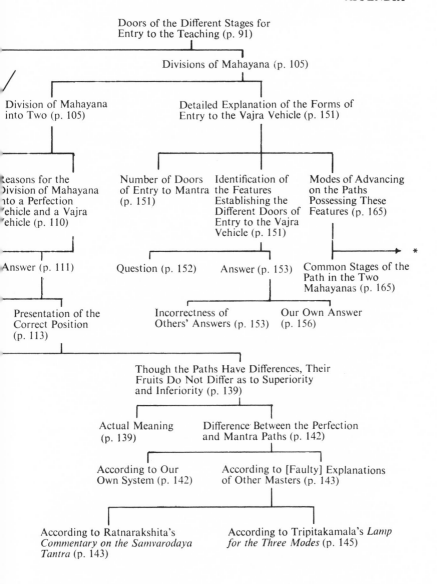

Doors of the Different Stages for
Entry to the Teaching (p. 91)

Divisions of Mahayana (p. 105)

Division of Mahayana
into Two (p. 105)

Detailed Explanation of the Forms of
Entry to the Vajra Vehicle (p. 151)

Reasons for the
Division of Mahayana
into a Perfection
Vehicle and a Vajra
Vehicle (p. 110)

Number of Doors
of Entry to Mantra
(p. 151)

Identification of
the Features
Establishing the
Different Doors of
Entry to the Vajra
Vehicle (p. 151)

Modes of Advancing
on the Paths
Possessing These
Features (p. 165)

Answer (p. 111)

Question (p. 152)

Answer (p. 153)

Common Stages of the
Path in the Two
Mahayanas (p. 165)

*

Presentation of the
Correct Position
(p. 113)

Incorrectness of
Others' Answers (p. 153)

Our Own Answer
(p. 156)

Though the Paths Have Differences, Their
Fruits Do Not Differ as to Superiority
and Inferiority (p. 139)

Actual Meaning
(p. 139)

Difference Between the Perfection
and Mantra Paths (p. 142)

According to Our
Own System (p. 142)

According to [Faulty] Explanations
of Other Masters (p. 143)

According to Ratnarakshita's
Commentary on the Samvarodaya
Tantra (p. 143)

According to Tripitakamala's Lamp
for the Three Modes (p. 145)

*The present translation ends at this point.

Glossary

English	Sanskrit	Tibetan
Action Seal	karmamudrā	las kyi phyag rgya
Action Tantra	kriyātantra	bya rgyud
affirming negative	paryudāsapratiṣhedha	ma yin dgag
affliction	klesha	nyon mongs
artificial	parikalpita	kun btags
bliss	sukha	bde ba
calm abiding	shamatha	zhi gnas
Cause Vehicle	hetuyāna	rgyu'i theg pa
Chittamatra	chittamātra	sems tsam
clarification	abhisaṃbodhi	mngon byang
compassion	karuṇā	snying rje
Complete Enjoyment Body	saṃbhogakāya	longs spyod rdzogs pa'i sku
concentration	dhyāna	bsam gtan
conception of self	ātmagrāha	bdag tu 'dzin pa
Conqueror	jina	rgyal ba
continuum	saṃtāna	rgyud
conventional truth	saṃvṛti satya	kun rdzob bden pa
cyclic existence	saṃsāra	'khor ba
definite goodness	niḥshreyasa	nges legs
Definition Vehicle	lakṣhaṇayāna	mtshan nyid kyi theg pa
definitive	nitārtha	nges don
deity yoga	devayoga	lha'i rnal 'byor
dependent-arising	pratītyasamutpāda	rten 'byung
desire realm	kāmadhātu	'dod khams
direct perception	pratyakṣha	mngon sum
discipline	vinaya	'dul ba
Effect Vehicle	phalayāna	'bras bu'i theg pa
effort	vīrya	brtson 'grus
elaborations	prapañcha	spros pa
element	dhātu	khams
Emanation Body	nirmāṇakāya	sprul pa'i sku
emptiness	shūnyatā	stong pa nyid
enlightenment	bodhi	byang chub
ethics	shīla	tshul khrims
expanse	dhātu	dbyings

faculty	indriya	dbang po
five aggregates	pañchaskandha	phung po lnga
Foe Destroyer	arhan	sgra bcom pa
Forder	tīrthika	mu stegs pa
Form Body	rūpakāya	gzugs sku
form realm	rūpadhātu	gzugs khams
formless realm	ārūpyadhātu	gzugs med khams
fruit	phala	'bras bu

generality	pradhāna	spyi
giving	dāna	sbyin pa
great compassion	mahākaruṇā	snying rje chen po
Great Seal	mahāmudrā	phyag rgya chen po
ground	bhūmi	sa

Hearer	shrāvaka	nyan thos
high status	abhyudaya	mngon mtho
Highest Yoga Tantra	anuttarayogatantra	rnal 'byor bla med kyi rgyud

illusory body	māyādeha	sgyu lus
individual emancipation	pratimokṣha	so sor thar pa
inference	anumāṇa	rjes dpag
inherent existence	svabhāvasiddhi	rang bzhin gyis grub pa
initiation	abhiṣheka	dbang
innate	sahaja	lhan skyes

Joyous Land	tuṣhita	dga' ldan

knowledge	abhidharma	chos mngon pa
Knowledge Woman	vidyā	rig ma

Land of Controlling Others' Emanations	paranirmitashavartin	gzhan 'phrul dbang byed
Land of Liking Emanation	nirmāṇarati	'phrul dga'
Land of the Thirty-Three	trāyastriṃsha	sum bcu rtsa gsum
Land Without Combat	yāma	'thab bral
liberation	mokṣha	thar pa
lineage	gotra	rigs
lord	īshvara	dbang phyug
love	maitri	byams pa

221

Madhyamika	mādhyamika	dbu ma pa
Mantra Vehicle	mantrayāna	sngags kyi theg pa
meditative equipoise	samāhita	mnyam bzhag
meditative stabilisation	samādhi	ting nge 'dzin
mental and physical aggregates	skandha	phung po
merit	puṇya	bsod nams
method	upāya	thabs
Method Vehicle	upāyayāna	thabs kyi theg pa
migrator	gati	'gro ba
mind of enlightenment	bodhichitta	byang chub kyi sems

natural existence	svalakṣhaṇasiddhi	rang gi mtshan nyid kyis grub pa
natural nirvana	svabhāvanirvāṇa	rang bzhin myang 'das
Nature Truth Body	svabhāvikakāya	ngo bo nyid sku
non-affirming negative	prasajyapratiṣhedha	med dgag
non-product	asaṃskṛta	'dus ma byas

obstructions to liberation/afflictive obstructions	kleshāvaraṇa	nyon mong pa'i sgrib pa
obstructions to omniscience	jñeyāvaraṇa	shes bya'i sgrib pa
omniscience	sarvākārajñāna	rnam pa thams cad mkhyen pa

path	mārga	lam
path of accumulation	saṃbhāramārga	tshogs lam
path of meditation	bhāvanāmārga	sgom lam
path of no more learning	ashaikṣhamārga	mi slob lam
path of preparation	prayogamārga	sbyor lam
path of seeing	darshanamārga	mthong lam
patience	kṣhānti	bzod pa
perfection	pāramitā	pha rol tu phyin pa
Perfection Vehicle	pāramitāyāna	phar phyin gyi theg pa
Performance Tantra	charyātantra	spyod rgyud
person	pudgala	gang zag
phenomenon	dharma	chos
Pledge Seal	samayamudrā	dam tshig gi phyag rgya
predisposition	vāsanā	bag chags
product	saṃskṛta	'dus byas

| repetition | jāpa | bzlas brjod |
| requiring interpretation | neyārtha | drang don |

222

Sautrantika	sautrāntika	mdo sde pa
Sautrantika-Svatantrika-Madhyamika	sautrāntika-svātantrika-mādhyamika	mdo sde spyod pa'i dbu ma rang rgyud pa
Scriptural Division of the Knowledge Bearers	vidhyādhārapiṭaka	rig 'dzin gyi sde snod
Seal	mudrā	phyag rgya
Secret Mantra Vehicle	guhyamantrayāna	gsang sngags kyi theg pa
selflessness	nairātmya	bdag med
selflessness of persons	pudgalanairātmya	gang zag gi bdag med
selflessness of phenomena	dharmanairātmya	chos kyi bdag med
sentient being	sattva	sems can
sets of discourses	sūtrānta	mdo sde
Sky-Goer	ḍākinī	mkha' 'gro
Solitary Realiser	pratyekabuddha	rang sangs rgyas
special insight	vipashyanā	lhag mthong
stage of completion	niṣhpannakrama	rdzogs rim
stage of generation	utpattikrama	bskyed rim
substantial existence	dravyasat	rdzas su yod pa
suchness	tathatā	de kho na nyid
Superior	āryan	'phags pa
suspicion/doubt	saṃshaya/vichikitsā	the tshom
symbolic being	samayasattva	dam tshig pa

Tathagata essence	tathāgatagarbha	de bzhin gshegs pa'i snying po
tenet/system of tenets	siddhānta	grub mtha'
Three Refuges	trisharana	skyabs gsum
Truth Body	dharmakāya	chos sku

ultimate truth	paramārthasatya	don dam bden pa
Universal Monarch	chakravartin	'khor sgyur
unusual attitude	adhyāshaya	lhag bsam

Vaibhashika	vaibhāṣhika	bye brag smra ba
valid cognition	pramāṇa	tshad ma
vehicle	yāna	theg pa
view of the transitory collection	satkāyadṛṣhṭi	'jig tshogs la lta ba

223

wind	prāṇa	rlung
wisdom	prajñā	shes rab
Wisdom Knowledge Woman	jñānavidyā	ye shes kyi rig ma
Wisdom Seal	jñānamudrā	ye shes kyi phyag rgya
Wisdom Truth Body	jñānadharmakāya	ye shes chos sku
wrong view	mithyādṛṣhṭi	log lta
Yoga Tantra	yogatantra	rnal 'byor rgyud
yoga with signs	sanimittayoga	mtshan bcas kyi rnal 'byor
yoga without signs	animittayoga	mtshan ma med pa'i rnal 'byor
Yogachara-Svatantrika-Madhyamika	yogāchara-svātantrika-mādhyamika	rnal 'byor spyod pa'i dbu ma rang rgyud pa

Bibliography

In the first section the titles are arranged alphabetically according to the English, followed by the Sanskrit and Tibetan; in the second section, by author. Here and in the notes, for works found in the Tibetan canon 'P' refers to the *Tibetan Tripitaka* (Tokyo-Kyoto, Suzuki Research Foundation, 1955), which is a reprint of the Peking edition. 'Toh.' refers either to *A Complete Catalogue of the Tibetan Buddhist Canons*, edited by Prof. Hakuji Ui *et al.* (Sendai, Japan, 1934) or to *A Catalogue of the Tohoku University Collection of Tibetan Works on Buddhism*, edited by Prof. Yensho Kanakura *et al.* (Sendai, Japan, 1953). 'Cone' refers to the *Co ne bstan 'gyur* in microfiche form as provided by the Institute for Advanced Studies of World Religions. The English titles are usually abbreviated.

I *Sutras and Tantras*

All Secret Tantra
Sarvarahasyanāmatantrarāja
Thams cad gsang ba rgyud kyi rgyal po
P114, vol. 5 (Toh. 481)

Appearances Shining as Vajras
sNang ba rdo rjer 'char ba
(Not found in either P or Toh.)

Brief Explication of Initiations
Shekhoddesha
dBang mdor bstan pa
P3, vol. 1 (Toh. 361)

Chapter of the True One Sutra
Satyakaparivartasūtra
bDen pa po'i le'u'i mdo
(Not found in either P or Toh.)

Compendium of All the Weaving Sutra
Sarvavaidalyasaṃgraha
rNam par 'thag pa thams cad bsdus pa
P893, vol. 35 (Toh. 227)

Compendium of the Principles of All Tathagatas
Sarvatathāgatatattvasaṃgrahanāmamahāyānasūtra
De bzhin gshegs pa thams cad kyi de kho na nyid bsdus pa zhes bya ba theg
pa chen po'i mdo
P112, vol. 4 (Toh. 479)

Compendium of Wisdom Vajras
Jñanavajrasamuchchayanāmatantra
Ye shes rdo rje kun las btus pa
P84, vol. 3 (Toh. 447)

225

TANTRA IN TIBET

Condensed Perfection of Wisdom Sutra
Sañchayagāthāprajñāpāramitāsūtra
Shes rab kyi pha rol tu phyin pa sdud pa tshigs su bcad pa
P735, vol. 21 (Toh. 13)

Detailed Rite of Amoghapasha
Amoghapāshakalparāja
Don yod pa'i zhags pa'i cho ga zhib mo'i rgyal po
P365, vol. 8 (Toh. 686)

Eight Thousand Stanza Perfection of Wisdom Sutra
Aṣhṭasāhasrikāprajñāpāramitāsūtra
Shes rab kyi pha rol tu phyin pa brgyad stong pa'i mdo
P734, vol. 21 (Toh. 12)

Expression of the Ultimate Names of the Wisdom-Being Manjushri
Mañjushrījñānasattvasya paramārthanāmasaṃgīti
'Jam dpal ye shes sems dpa'i don dam pa'i mtshan yang dag par brjod pa
P2, vol. 1 (Toh. 360)

Guhyasamaja Tantra
Sarvatathāgatakāyavākcittarahasyaguhyasamājanāmamahākalparāja
De bzhin gshegs pa thams cad kyi sku gsung thugs kyi gsang chen gsang ba
'dus pa zhes bya ba brtag pa'i rgyal po chen po
P81, vol. 3 (Toh. 442–3)

Hevajra Tantra
Hevajratantrarāja
Kye'i rdo rje zhes bya ba rgyud kyi rgyal po
P10, vol. 1 (Toh. 417–8)

Introduction to the Forms of Definite and Indefinite Progress Sutra
Niyatāniyatagatimudrāvatāra
Nges pa dang mi nges par 'gro ba'i phyag rgya la 'jug pa
P868, vol. 34 (Toh. 202)

Kalachakra Tantra
Paramādibuddhoddhṛtashrīkālachakranāmatantrarāja
mChog gi dang po'i sangs rgyas las byung ba rgyud kyi rgyal po dpal dus
kyi 'khor lo
P4, vol. 1 (Toh. 362)

Kashyapa Chapter Sutra
Kāshyapaparivartasūtra
'Od srung gi le'u'i mdo
P760. 43, vol. 24 (Toh. 87)

Little Samvara Tantra
Tantrarājashrīlaghusaṃvara
rGyud kyi rgyal po dpal bde mchog nyung ngu'i rgyud
P16, vol. 2 (Toh. 368)

Meeting of Father and Son Sutra
Pitāputrasamāgamasūtra
Yab dang sras mjal ba'i mdo
P760. 16, vol. 23 (Toh. 60)

226

Ornament of the Vajra Essense Tantra
Vajrahṛdayālaṃkāratantra
rDo rje snying po rgyan gyi rgyud
P86, vol. 3 (Toh. 451)

Paramadya Tantra
Shrīparamādyanāmamahāyānakalparāja
dPal mchog dang po zhes bya ba theg pa chen po'i rtog pa'i rgyal po
P119, vol. 5 (Toh. 487)

Questions of Subahu Tantra
Subāhupariprchchhānāmatantra
dPung bzang gis zhus pa zhes bya ba'i rgyud
P428, vol. 9 (Toh. 805)

Samputa Tantra
Saṃpuṭanāmamahātantra
Yang dag par sbyor ba zhes bya ba'i rgyud
P26, vol. 2 (Toh. 381)

Sutra of the Wise Man and the Fool
Damamūkonāmasūtra
mDzangs blun zhes bya ba'i mdo
P1008, vol. 40 (Toh. 341)

Sutra Revealing the Secret
gSang ba lung bstan pa'i mdo
(Not found in either P or Toh.)

Vairochanabhisambodhi Tantra
Mahāvairochanābhisaṃbodhivikurvatī-adhiṣhṭhānavaipulyaparyāya
rNam par snang mdzad chen po mngon par rdzogs par byang chub pa rnam
    par sprul ba byin gyis rlob pa shin tu rgyas pa mdo sde'i dbang po rgyal po
    zhes bya ba'i chos kyi rnam grangs
P126, vol. 5 (Toh. 494)

Vajradaka Tantra
Vajraḍākaguhyatantrarāja
rDo rje mkha' 'gro gsang ba'i rgyud kyi rgyal po
P44, vol. 3 (Toh. 399)

Vajrapani Initiation Tantra
Vajrapāṇyabhiṣhekamahātantra
Lag na rdo rje dbang bskur ba'i rgyud chen mo
P130, vol. 6 (Toh. 496)

Vajrapanjara Tantra
Ḍākinīvajrapañjaramahātantrarājakalpa
mKha' 'gro ma rdo rje gur zhes bya ba'i rgyud kyi rgyal po chen po'i brtag
pa
P11, vol. 1 (Toh. 419)

Vajrashekhara Tantra
Vajrashekharamahāguhyayogatantra
gSang ba rnal 'byor chen po'i rgyud rdo rje rtse mo
P113, vol. 5 (Toh. 480)

227

TANTRA IN TIBET

Vishnu Tantra
Khyab 'jug gi rgyud
(Not found in either P or Toh.)
White Lotus of the Excellent Doctrine
Saddharmapuṇḍarīkasūtra
Dam pa'i chos pad ma dkar po'i mdo
P781, vol. 30 (Toh. 113)

II *Other Works*

Abhayākaraguptapāda ('Jig-med-'byung-gnas-kyi-sbas-pa)
Clusters of Quintessential Instructions,
A Commentary on the Samputa Tantra
Saṃpuṭatantrarājaṭīkā-āmnāyamañjari
Yang dag par sbyor ba'i rgyud kyi rgyal po'i rgya cher 'grel pa man ngag gi snye ma
P2328, vol. 55 (Toh. 1198)
Alaṃkakalasha
Commentary on the Vajra Garland Tantra
Vajramālāmahāyogatantraṭīkāgambhīrārthadīpikā
rNal 'byor chen po'i rgyud dpal rdo rje phreng ba'i rgya cher 'grel pa zab mo'i don gyi 'grel pa
P2660, vol. 61 (Toh. 1795)
Ānandagarbha (Kun-dga'-snying-po)
Commentary on the Guhyasamaja Tantra
Guhyasamājamahātantrarājaṭīkā
rGyud kyi rgyal po chen po dpal gsang ba 'dus pa'i rgya cher 'grel pa
P4787, vol. 84 (Toh. 1917)
Illumination of the 'Compendium of Principles'
Sarvatathāgatatattvasaṃgrahamahāyānābhisamayanāmatantravyākhyā-tattvālokakarī
De bzhin gshegs pa thams cad kyi de kho na nyid bsdus pa theg pa chen po mngon par rtogs pa zhes bya ba'i rgyud kyi bshad pa de kho na nyid snang bar byed pa
P3333, vol. 71–2 (Toh. 2510)
Āryadeva ('Phags-pa-lha)
Four Hundred/Treatise of Four Hundred Stanzas
Chatuḥshatakashāstrakārikā
bsTan bcos bzhi brgya pa zhes bya ba'i tshig le'ur byas pa
P5246, vol. 95 (Toh. 3846)
Lamp Compendium of Practice
Charyāmelāpakapradīpa
sPyod pa bsdus pa'i sgron ma
P2668, vol. 61 (Toh. 1803)

Asaṅga (Thogs-med)
Five Treatises on the Levels
Levels of Yogic Practice/Actuality of the Levels
Yogacharyābhūmi
rNal 'byor spyod pa'i sa
P5536–8, vol. 109–10 (Toh. 4035–7)
Compendium of Ascertainments
Nirṇayasaṃgraha
gTan la dbab pa bsdu ba
P5539, vol. 110–11 (Toh. 4038)
Compendium of Bases
Vastusaṃgraha
bZhi bsdu ba
P5540, vol. 111 (Toh. 4039)
Compendium of Enumerations
Paryāyasaṃgraha
rNam grang bsdu ba
P5542, vol. 111 (Toh. 4041)
Compendium of Explanations
Vivaraṇasaṃgraha
rNam par bshad pa bsdu ba
P5543, vol. 111 (Toh. 4042)
Ashvaghoṣha (rTa-dbyangs)
Fifty Stanzas on the Guru
Gurupañchāshikā
bLa ma lnga bcu pa
P4544, vol. 81 (Toh. 3721)
Twenty Stanzas on the Bodhisattva Vow
Bodhisattvasaṃvaravimshaka
Byang chub sems dpa'i sdom pa nyi shu pa
P5582, vol. 114 (Toh. 4081)
Bhavabhadra
Commentary on the Vajradaka Tantra
Shrīvajraḍākanāmamahātantrarājasya vivṛti
rGyud kyi rgyal po chen po dpal rdo rje mkha' 'gro zhes bya ba'i rnam par
bshad pa
P2131, vol. 50 (Toh. 1415)
Buddhaguhya (Sangs-rgyas-gsang-ba)
Condensation of the Questions of Subahu Tantra
Subāhupariprchchhānāmatantrapiṇḍārtha
dPung bzang gis zhus pa'i rgyud kyi bsdus pa'i don
P3496, vol. 78 (Toh. 2671)
Condensation of the Vairochanabhisambodhi Tantra
Vairochanābhisaṃbodhitantrapiṇḍārtha
rNam par snang mdzad mngon par rdzogs par byang chub pa'i rgyud kyi
bsdus pa'i don
P3486, vol. 77 (Toh. 2662)

229

Word Commentary on the Vairochanabhisambodhi Tantra
Vairochanābhisaṃbodhivikurvitādhiṣhṭhānamahātantrabhāṣhya
rNam par snang mdzad mngon par byang chub pa rnam par sprul pa'i byin
gyis brlabs kyi rgyud chen po'i bshad pa
P3487, vol. 77 (Toh. 2663)
Bu-tön (Bu-ston)
    *Condensed General Presentation of the Tantra Sets, Key Opening the Door
    of the Precious Treasury of Tantra Sets*
    rGyud sde spyi'i rnam bzhag bsdus pa rgyud sde rin po che'i gter sgo 'byed
    pa'i lde mig
    Collected Works, Part 14 pha (New Delhi, International Academy of Indian
    Culture, 1969), (Toh. 5167)
    *Extensive General Presentation of the Tantra Sets, Jewelled Adornment of
    the Tantra Sets*
    rGyud sde spyi'i rnam par gzhag pa rgyud sde rin po che'i mdzes rgyan
    Collected Works, Part 15 ba (New Delhi, International Academy of Indian
    Culture, 1969), (Toh. 5169)
    *Middling General Presentation of the Tantra Sets, Illuminating the Secrets
    of All Tantra Sets*
    rGyud sde spyi'i rnam par gzhag pa rgyud sde thams cad kyi gsang ba gsal
    bar byed pa zhes bya ba
    Collected Works, Part 15 ba (New Delhi, International Academy of Indian
    Culture, 1969), (Toh. 5168)
Chandrakīrti (Zla-ba-grags-pa)
    Commentary to 'A Supplement to the Middle Way'
    Madhyamakāvatārabhāṣhya
    dbU ma la 'jug pa'i bshad pa
    P5263, vol. 98 (Toh. 3862)
    Supplement to the Middle Way
    Madhyamakāvatāra
    dbU ma la 'jug pa
    P5262 and 5261, vol. 98. (Toh. 3861)
Devakulamahāmati (Lha-rigs-kyi-blo-gros-chen-po)
    Commentary on the Difficult Points of the Vajrapanjara Tantra
    Ḍākinīvajrajālapañjaratantrarājasya pañjikāpauṣhtika
    rGyud kyi rgyal po mkha' 'gro ma rdo rje dra ba'i dka' 'grel de kho na nyid
    rgyas pa
    P2326, vol. 54 (Toh. 1196)
Dharmakīrti (Chos-kyi-grags-pa)
    Seven Treatises on Valid Cognition
        Commentary on (Dignaga's) 'Compendium of Valid Cognition'
        Pramāṇavarttikakārikā
        Tshad ma rnam 'grel gyi tshig le'ur byas pa
        P5709, vol. 130 (Toh. 4210)
        Ascertainment of Valid Cognition
        Pramāṇavinishchaya
        Tshad ma rnam par nges pa

P5710, vol. 130 (Toh. 4211)
Drop of Reasoning
Nyāyabinduprakaraṇa
Rigs pa'i thigs pa zhes bya ba'i rab tu byed pa
P5711, vol. 130 (Toh. 4212)
Drop of Reasons
Hetubindunāmaprakaraṇa
gTan tshigs kyi thigs pa zhes bya ba rab tu byed pa
P5712, vol. 130 (Toh. 4213)
Analysis of Relations
Saṃbandhaparīkṣhāvṛtti
'Brel pa brtag pa'i rab tu byed pa
P5713, vol. 130 (Toh. 4214)
Reasoning for Debate
Vādanyāyanāmaprakaraṇa
rTsod pa'i rigs pa zhes bya ba'i rab tu byed pa
P5715, vol. 130 (Toh. 4218)
Proof of Other Continuums
Samṭānāntarasiddhināmaprakaraṇa
rGyud gzhan grub pa zhes bya ba'i rab tu byed pa
P5716, vol. 130 (Toh. 4219)

Durjayachandra (Mi-thub-zla-ba)
Commentary on the Difficult Points of the Hevajra Tantra
Kaumudīnāmapañjikā
Kau mu dī zhes bya ba'i dka' 'grel
P2315, vol. 53 (Toh. 1185)

Gyel-tsap (rGyal-tshab)
Essence of the Good Expositions, An Explanation of (Aryadeva's) 'Four
Hundred'
bZhi brgya pa'i rnam bshad legs bshad snying po
(Blockprint in the Dalai Lama's library; place and date of
publication unknown.)

Indrabodhi (or Indrabhūti)
Commentary on the Difficult Points of the Vajrapanjara Tantra
Ḍākinīvajrapañjaramahātantrarājasya pañjikāprathamapaṭalamukhabandha
rGyud kyi rgyal po mkha' 'gro ma rdo rje gur gyi dka' 'grel zhal nas brgyud
pa
P2324, vol. 54 (Toh. 1194)

Jam-yang-shay-ba ('Jam-dbyangs-bzhad-pa)
Great Exposition of Tenets/A Presentation of Tenets, the Roar of the
Five-Faced (Lion) Eradicating Error, A Precious Lamp Illuminating the
Good Path to Omniscience
Grub mtha'i rnam par bzhag pa 'khrul spong gdong lnga'i sgra dbyangs kun
mkhyen lam bzang gsal ba'i rin chen sgron me
(New Delhi, Guru Deva)
Great Exposition of the Middle Way/Analysing the Limits of Pervasion in
(Chandrakirti's) 'Supplement to the Treatise on the Middle Way', A

231

Treasury of Scripture and Reasoning, Thoroughly Illuminating the Profound Meaning of Emptiness, An Entrance for the Fortunate
dbU ma la 'jug pa'i mtha' dpyod lung rigs gter mdzod zab don kun gsal skal bzang 'jug ngog
(Buxaduor, Gomang, 1967)

Jang-kya (lCang-skya)
Presentation of Tenets/Clear Exposition of the Presentations of Tenets, A Beautiful Ornament for the Meru of the Subduer's Teaching
Grub pa'i mtha'i rnam par bzhag pa gsal bar bshad pa thub bstan lhun po'i mdzes rgyan
(Varanasi, The Pleasure of Elegant Sayings Printing Press, 1970)

Jinadatta (rGyal-bas-byin)
Commentary on the Difficult Points of the Guhyasamaja Tantra
Guhyasamājatantrapañjikā
dPal gsang ba 'dus pa'i rgyud kyi dka' 'grel
P2710, vol. 63 (Toh. 1847)

Jñānakīrti (Ye-shes-grags-pa)
Abridged Explanation of All the Word of the Sugata
Tattvāvatārākhyasakalasugatavachastātparyavyākhyāprakaraṇa
De kho na nyid la 'jug pa zhes bya ba bde bar gshegs pa'i bka' ma lus pa mdor bsdus ste bshad pa'i rab tu byed pa
P4532, vol. 81 (Toh. 3709)

Jñānapāda (Ye-shes-zhabs)
Engaging in the Means of Self-Achievement
Ātmasādhanāvatāra
bDag sgrub pa la 'jug pa
P2723, vol. 65 (Toh. 1860)

Jñānashrī (Ye-shes-dpal)
Eradication of the Two Extremes in the Vajra Vehicle
Vajrayānakoṭidvayāpoha
rDo rje theg pa'i mtha' gnyis sel ba
P4537, vol. 81 (Toh. 3714)

Kön-chok-jig-may-wang-po (dKon-mchog-'jigs-med-dbang-po)
Precious Garland of Tenets/Presentation of Tenets, A Precious Garland
Grub pa'i mtha'i rnam par bzhag pa rin po che'i phreng ba
(Dharamsala, Shes-rig-par-khang, 1969)

Kṛṣhṇapāda (Nag-po-zhabs)
Explanation of the Vajrapanjara Tantra
Ḍākinīvajrapañjaranāmamahātantrarājakalpamukhabandha
mKha' 'gro ma rdo rje gur zhes bya ba'i rgyud kyi rgyal po chen po'i rtag pa'i rgyal po'i bshad sbyar
P2325, vol. 54 (Toh. 1195)

Long-chen-rap-jam (kLong-chen-rab-'byams/kLong-chen-pa Dri-med-'od-zer).
Precious Treasury of the Supreme Vehicle
Theg pa'i mchog rin po che'i mdzod
(Gangtok, Dodrup Chen Rinpoche, 1969 (?))

BIBLIOGRAPHY

Treasury of Tenets, Illuminating the Meaning of All Vehicles
Theg pa mtha' dag gi don gsal bar byed pa grub pa'i mtha' rin po che'i
mdzod
(Gangtok, Dodrup Chen Rinpoche, 1969 (?))
Long-dol Ngak-wang-lo-sang (kLong-rdol Ngag-dbang-blo-bzang)
*Terminology Arising in Secret Mantra, the Scriptural Division of the
Knowledge Bearers*
gSang sngags rig pa 'dzin pa'i sde snod las byung ba'i ming gi grang
The Collected Works of Longdol Lama Parts 1 and 2 (New Delhi,
International Academy of Indian Culture, 1973)
Lo-sang-chö-ki-gyel-tsen (bLo-bzang-chos-kyi-rgyal-mtshan)
Presentation of the General Teaching and the Four Tantra Sets
bsTan pa spyi dang rgyud sde bzhi'i rnam par gzhag pa'i zin bris
Collected Works, vol. 4 (New Delhi, Gurudeva, 1973)
Maitreya (Byams-pa)
Ornament for the Mahayana Sutras
Mahāyānasūtrālaṃkārakārikā
Theg pa chen po'i mdo sde'i rgyan gyi tshig le'ur byas pa
P5521, vol. 108 (Toh. 4020)
Ornament for the Realisations
Abhisamayālaṃkāra
mNgon par rtogs pa'i rgyan
P5184, vol. 88 (Toh. 3786)
Mātṛcheta and Dignāga (Phyogs-kyi-glang-po)
Interwoven Praise
Mishrakastotra
sPel mar bstod pa
P2041, vol. 46 (Toh. 1150)
Nāgārjuna (kLu-sgrub)
Collections of Reasoning
  *Treatise on the Middle Way/Fundamental Stanzas on the Middle
    Way Called 'Wisdom'*
  Prajñānāmamūlamadhyamakakārikā/Madhyamakashāstra
  dbU ma rtsa ba'i tshig le'ur byas pa shes rab ces bya ba
  P5224, vol. 95 (Toh. 3824)
  Sixty Stanzas of Reasoning
  Yuktiṣhaṣhṭikākārikā
  Rigs pa drug cu pa'i tshig le'ur byas pa
  P5225, vol. 95 (Toh. 3825)
  Treatise Called 'The Finely Woven'
  Vaidalyasūtranāma
  Zhib mo rnam par 'thag pa zhes bya ba'i mdo
  P5226, vol. 95 (Toh. 3826)
  Seventy Stanzas on Emptiness
  Shūnyatāsaptatikārikā
  sTong pa nyid bdun cu pa'i tshig le'ur byas pa
  P5227, vol. 95 (Toh. 3827)

233

Refutation of Objections
Vigrahavyāvartanīkārikā
rTsod pa bzlog pa'i tshig le'ur byas pa
P5228, vol. 95 (Toh. 3828)
Praise of the Non-Conceptual
Nirvikalpastava (?)
rNam par mi rtog par bstod pa
(Not found in P or Toh.)
Precious Garland of Advice for the King
Rājaparikathāratnāvalī
rGyal po la gtam bya ba rin po che'i phreng ba
P5658, vol. 129 (Toh. 4158)
Pa-bong-ka-pa (Pha-bong-kha-pa)
*Miscellaneous Notes from Jo-nay Pandita's Explanation of the Great
Exposition of Secret Mantra*
rJe btsun bla ma co ne paṇḍi ta rin po che'i zhal snga nas sngags rim chen
mo'i bshad lung nos skabs kyi gsung bshad zin bris thor tsam du bkod pa
Collected Works, Volume 2 (New Delhi, Chophel Legdan, 1972)
Pad-ma-kar-po (Pad-ma-dkar-po)
General Presentation of the Tantra Sets, Captivating the Wise
rGyud sde spyi'i rnam gzhag mkhas pa'i yid 'phrog
Collected Works, Volume 11 (Darjeeling, Kargyud Sungrab Nyamso
Khang, 1974)
Rāhulashrīmitra (sGra-gcan-'dzin-dpal-bshes-gnyen)
Clarification of Union
Yuganaddhaprakāshanāmasekaprakriyā
Zung du 'jug pa gsal ba zhes bya ba'i dbang gi bya ba
P2682, vol. 62 (Toh. 1818)
Ratnākarashānti (Shāntipa or Rin-chen-'byung-gnas-zhi-ba)
Commentary on the Difficult Points of the Hevajra Tantra
Hevajrapañjikāmuktikāvalī
dGyes pa'i rdo rje'i dka' 'grel mu tig phreng ba
P2319, vol. 54 (Toh. 1189)
Commentary on (Dipankarabhadra's) 'Four Hundred and Fifty'
Guhyasamājamaṇḍalavidhiṭīkā
dPal gsang ba 'dus pa'i dkyil 'khor gyi cho ga'i 'grel pa
P2734, vol. 65 (Toh. 1871)
Handful of Flowers, Explanation of the Guhyasamaja Tantra
Kusumāñjaliguhyasamājanibandha
gSang ba 'dus pa'i bshad sbyar snyim pa'i me tog
P2714, vol. 64 (Toh. 1851)
Presentation of the Three Vehicles
Triyānavyavasthāna
Theg pa gsum rnam par bzhag pa
P4535, vol. 81 (Toh. 3712)
Ratnarakṣhita
Commentary on the Difficult Points of the Samvarodaya Tantra

Saṃvarodayamahātantrarājasya padminīnāmapañjikā
sDom pa 'byung ba'i rgyud kyi rgyal po chen po'i dka' 'grel
P2137, vol. 51 (Toh. 1420)

Rig-den-pad-ma-kar-po (Rigs-ldan-pad-ma-dkar-po)
Stainless Light
Vimālaprabhānāmamūlatantrānusāriṇīdvādashasāhasrikālaghukālachakratantrarājaṭīkā
bsDus pa'i rgyud kyi rgyal po dus kyi 'khor lo'i 'grel bshad rtsa ba'i rgyud
kyi rjes su 'jug pa stong phrag bcu gnyis pa dri ma med pa'i 'od ces bya ba
P2064, vol. 46 (Toh. 845)

Samayavajra (Dam-tshig-rdo-rje)
Commentary on the Krshnayamari Tantra
Kṛṣhṇayamāritantrarājāprekṣhaṇapathapradīpanāmaṭīkā
gShin rje gshed nag po'i rgyud kyi rgyal po mngon par mthong ba lam gyi
sgron ma zhes bya ba'i rgya cher bshad pa
P2783, vol. 66 (Toh. 1920)

Seventh Dalai Lama Kaysang Gyatso (bsKal-bzang-rgya-mtsho)
Explanation of the Rite of the Guhyasamaja Mandala
gSang 'dus dkyil 'khor cho ga'i rnam bshad
(New Delhi, Tanzin Kunga, 1972)

Shākyamitra (Shākya'i-bshes-gnyen)
Ornament of Kosala, Commentary on the 'Compendium of Principles'
Kosalālaṃkāratattvasaṃgrahaṭīkā
De kho na nyid bsdus pa'i rgya cher bshad pa ko sa la'i rgyan
P3326, vol. 70–71 (Toh. 2503)

Shaṃkarapati (bDe-byed-bdag-po)
Praise of the Supra-Divine
Devātishayastotra
Lha las phul du byung bar bstod pa
P2004, vol. 46 (Toh. 1112)

Shāntideva (Zhi-ba-lha)
Engaging in the Bodhisattva Deeds
Bodhisattvacharyāvatāra
Byang chub sems dpa'i spyod pa la 'jug pa
P5272, vol. 99 (Toh. 3871)

Shāntirakṣhita (Zhi-ba-'tsho)
Text on the Establishment of the Principles
Tattvasiddhināmaprakaraṇa
De kho na nyid grub pa zhes bya ba'i rab tu byed pa
P4531, vol. 81 (Toh. 3708)

Shraddhākaravarma
Introduction to the Meaning of the Highest Yoga Tantras
Yogānuttaratantrārthāvatārasaṃgraha
rNal 'byor bla med pa'i rgyud kyi don la 'jug pa bsdus pa
P4536, vol. 81 (Toh. 3713)

235

Shrīdhara (dPal-'dzin)
  Innate Illumination, Commentary on the Difficult Points of the Yamari
    Tantra
  Yamāritantrapañjikāsahajāloka
  gShin rje gshed kyi rgyud kyi dka' 'grel lhan cig skyes pa'i snang ba
  P2781, vol. 66 (Toh. 1918)

Sö-nam-tse-mo (bSod-nams-rtse-mo)
  General Presentation of the Tantra Sets
  rGyud sde spyi'i rnam par gzhag pa
  (sGang-tog, 'Bras-ljongs-sa-ngor-chos-tshogs, 1969)

Tak-tsang (sTag-tshang)
  An Explanation of 'Freedom from Extremes' in 'Revelation of All Tenets',
    An Ocean of Eloquence
  Grub mtha' kun shes nas mtha' bral grub pa zhes bya ba'i bstan bcos rnam
    par bshad pa legs bshad kyi rgya mtsho.
  (Photographic reprint in the possession of Khetsun Sangpo; place and date
    of publication unknown.)

Tripiṭakamāla
  Lamp for the Three Modes
  Nayatrayapradīpa
  Tshul gsum gyi sgron ma
  P4530, vol. 81 (Toh. 3707)

Tsong-ka-pa (Tsong-kha-pa)
  Door of Entry to the Seven Treatises, Dispelling the Mental Darkness of
    Seekers
  sDe bdun la 'jug pa'i sgo don gnyer yid kyi mun sel
  (Toh. 5416)
  Great Exposition of Secret Mantra/The Stages of the Path to a Conqueror
    and Pervasive Master, a Great Vajradhara: Revealing All Secret Topics
  rGyal ba khyab bdag rdo rje 'chang chen po'i lam gyi rim pa gsang ba kun
    gyi gnad rnam par phye ba
  P6210, vol. 161 (Toh. 5281)
  Great Exposition of the Stages of the Path Common to the Vehicles/Stages
    of the Path to Enlightenment Thoroughly Teaching All the Stages of
    Practice of the Three Types of Persons
  sKyes bu gsum gyi nyams su blang ba'i rim pa thams cad tshang bar ston
    pa'i byang chub lam gyi rim pa
  P6001, vol. 152 (Toh. 5392)

Vajragarbha (rDo-rje-snying-po)
  Commentary on the Condensation of the Hevajra Tantra
  Hevajrapiṇḍārthaṭīkā
  Kye'i rdo rje bsdus pa'i don gyi rgya cher 'grel pa
  P2310, vol. 53 (Toh. 1180)

Vinayadatta ('Dul-bas-byin)
  Rite of the Great Illusion Mandala
  Gurūpadeshanāmamahāmāyāmaṇḍalopāyika

sGyu 'phrul chen mo'i dkyil 'khor gyi cho ga bla ma'i zhal snga'i man ngag
    ces bya ba
P2517, vol. 57 (Toh. 1645)

Vīryavajra (dPa'-bo-rdo-rje)
Commentary on the Samputa Tantra
Sarvatantrasya nidānamahāguhyashrīsaṃpuṭanāmatantrarājaṭīkāratnamālā
rGyud thams cad kyi gleng gzhi dang gsang chen dpal kun tu kha sbyor zhes
    bya ba'i rgyud kyi rgyal po'i rgya cher bshad pa rin chen phreng ba zhes
    bya ba
P2329, vol. 55 (Toh. 1199)

Notes

For full Sanskrit and Tibetan titles see the bibliography.

1 Vajradhara. Knowledge mantras are mantras for the sake of abandoning ignorance and generating knowledge as well as for attaining clairvoyance and so forth.

2 sKyabs-mchog-dpal-bzang who also knew Sanskrit.

3 bSod-nams-bzang-po.

4 P2041, vol. 46, 87.5.2–87.5.6. Tsong-ka-pa has omitted a few lines without affecting the meaning.

5 Buddhas, literally 'those gone to bliss'.

6 P2004, vol. 46, 22.3.6.

7 Chapter I.

8 Chapter XII. Parenthetical additions are from Gyel-tsap's commentary *Essence of the Good Expositions, An Explanation of (Aryadeva's) 'Four Hundred'*, 90b.3–91a.3 (blockprint in the Dalai Lama's library).

9 See pp. 31-3.

10 His *sDe bdun la 'jug pa'i sgo don gnyer yid kyi mun sel* (Toh. 5416) has only a brief reference to the process, but his student Gyel-tsap wrote extensively on the topic in his commentary to Dharmakirti's *Ascertainment of Valid Cognition*.

11 See bibliography and pp. 35-6.

12 P2668, vol. 61, 311.1.7–311.2.1.

13 P4530, vol. 81, 119.3.3.

14 P4532, vol. 81, 125.2.7ff.

15 This and the next citation are quoted by Chandrakirti in his *Clear Words*, commenting on XVIII.5.

16 'Sugatas' and 'Kings of Doctrine' are Buddhas. 'Endurance' means facility with emptiness.

17 This is quoted by Chandrakirti in his *Clear Words*, commenting on I.3.

18 *Clear Words*, P5263, vol. 98, 43.5.7. 'Exists' refers to inherent existence; 'does not exist' refers to non-existence even conventionally.

19 See Bibliography pp. 233-4.

20 P868, vol. 34, 281.1.3ff. (1) Ox chariot: someone who tries to cross the world systems in an ox chariot, advances one hundred yojanas over a long time, but is turned back by winds. This is a Bodhisattva who either takes a liking to the Hinayana himself or causes others to do so, thus dulling his wisdom. (2) Elephant chariot: one who advances two thousand yojanas in a hundred years and also takes a liking to Hinayana. The complete enlightenment of these two is indefinite; they will turn back from the path of highest wisdom. (3) Sun and moon: one who

crosses the world systems over a long time in the manner of the sun and the moon. This is a Bodhisattva who devotes himself fully to Mahayana, not conjoining his wisdom with a lower motivation. (4) Magical creation of a Hearer: one who crosses the world systems in the manner of a Hearer's magical emanation, having even greater devotion to the Mahayana, its practitioners, and practices. (5) Magical creation of a Tathagata: one who wants to cross the world systems and petitions a Tathagata. This is a Bodhisattva who takes special care to set other sentient beings on the path. The complete enlightenment of these three is definite; they will not turn back from the path of highest wisdom.

21 This is quoted in Nagarjuna's *Compendium of Sutra*, P5330, vol. 102, 101.3.8ff.

22 P893, vol. 35, 124.5.4–124.5.7.

23 P893, vol. 35, 125.3.4–125.3.6.

24 P2, vol. 1, 121.3.3. This is quoted by Ratnakarashanti in his *Presentation of the Three Vehicles* (Cone: rGyud tsu 102b.7).

25 P4536, vol. 81, 154.5.7.

26 P4537, vol. 81, 159.3.4.

27 P81, vol. 3, 200.4.2. Man is explained as *manana* (minding) and *trā* as *trāṇana* (protecting). 'All vajras' refers to practitioners' body, speech, and mind. XVIII. 69c–71b.

28 P4536, vol. 81, 155.2.1.

29 The six branches as set forth in the *Kalachakra Tantra* are withdrawal, concentration, vitality and exertion, holding, mindfulness, and meditative stabilisation *(pratyāhāra, dhyāna, prāṇāyāma, dhāraṇā, anusmṛti, samādhi)*.

30 P4537, vol. 81, 159.3.7.

31 P4536, vol. 81, 155.2.3–155.2.7.

32 P81, vol. 3, 200.1.2–200.1.4.

33 See pp. 156–7, 161, and 201 for explanation of the stanza.

34 The white and red minds of enlightenment are the vital essences of male and female.

35 P11, vol. 1, 223.4.4–223.4.7.

36 P2326, vol. 54, 293.4.5–294.1.2.

37 P2326, vol. 54, 293.5.6.

38 P2325, vol. 54, 290.3.7–290.4.2.

39 P2324, vol. 54, 288.1.5–288.1.8. According to the Tohoku catalogue, his name is Indrabhūti.

40 P2326, vol. 54, 293.4.5–294.1.2.

41 P2723, vol. 65, 28.2.6–28.3.5.

42 This means to conceive enlightenment to exist concretely, or inherently.

43 P2723, vol. 65, 28.3.5.

44 P2723, vol. 65, 28.3.5.

45 P2723, vol. 65, 28.4.8.

46 P2723, vol. 65, 29.2.8–29.3.2.

47 P2723, vol. 65, 29.3.3.

48 P2734, vol. 65, 173.5.2–173.5.4.

49 P2328, vol. 55, 180.2.8–180.3.1.
50 P11, vol. 1, 235.2.8.
51 P11, vol. 1, 235.3.1. The Durjayachandra reference is to P2315, vol. 53, 272.4.4.
52 P2781, vol. 66, 219.4.4–219.4.8.
53 P2781, vol. 66, 219.4.8.
54 P114, vol. 5, 57.1.5.
55 P2783, vol. 66, 264.3.1–264.3.7.
56 P2710, vol. 63, 236.1.1ff.
57 P2517, vol. 57, 316.5.5–316.5.6.
58 P2723, vol. 65, 29.5.1ff.
59 P112, vol. 4, 237.5.7.
60 P3333, vol. 71, 151.4.6–151.4.7.
61 Cone: rGyud tsu 100b.2.
62 A life as a Universal Monarch is attained through special virtuous acts (see Nagarjuna's *Precious Garland* (London, George Allen & Unwin, 1975), verses 198–9), not through meditation imagining oneself as having the body and so forth of a Universal Monarch.
63 Cone: rGyud tsha 8a.6–8b.3.
64 Cone: rGyud tshu 26b.3.
65 P4530, vol. 81, 115.2.5–115.2.6; commentary until 118.2.6.
66 Cone: rGyud wa 46b.1 through 48a.1.
67 Cone: rGyud wa 47b.2.
68 The channels are passageways through which the drops—vital essences—course, impelled by the winds, or currents of energy.
69 See note 65. Tsong-ka-pa condenses Tripitakamala's own commentary, from which material has been added in brackets.
70 P4530, vol. 81, 117.5.5.
71 P4532, vol. 81, 133.2.1–133.4.7.
72 Knowledge Women (*Vidyā*) are so called because of being women in dependence on whom an original innate bliss consciousness cognising suchness is generated. Wisdom Knowledge Women (*Jñānavidyā*) are meditated or 'emanated' partners who are imagined in meditation, whereas external Knowledge Women are actual physical partners. Knowledge Women are also called Seals (*Mudrā*) because when in dependence on them a bliss consciousness cognising emptiness is generated, phenomena appear as the sport of this consciousness and are thus marked (or sealed) by it. Actual partners are called Pledge Seals (*Samayamudrā*) if fully qualified through (a) possessing the appropriate lineage, age, and so forth, (b) having ripened their mental continuum by the practice of the common path, and (c) keeping the tantric pledges. If not fully qualified, actual partners are called Action Seals (*Karmamudrā*), though Pledge Seals can also be called Action Seals from the point of view of actually engaging in the actions or deeds of desire. Meditated partners are called Wisdom Seals (*Jñānamudrā*) due to being manifestations, within deity yoga, of a wisdom consciousness cognising emptiness. The Great Seal (*Mahāmudrā*) to which

Tripitakamala referred on p. 146 is an indivisibility of wisdom and method and not either a meditated or actual woman. In his system, which is mistaken, inferior trainees rely on Action, Pledge, and Wisdom Seals in order to empower the mind in such a way that the Great Seal can be realised. Thus, according to him, the best of the superior trainees do not have desire for and do not use Action, Pledge, or Wisdom Seals.

73 As Tsong-ka-pa says in the next paragraph, neither Tripitakamala nor Jnanakirti specify the difference between Pledge and Action Seals. The bracketed addition here comes from the Lati Rinpochay.

74 P4532, vol. 81, 125.4.2–125.4.3.

75 P4532, vol. 81, 134.2.6–134.2.7.

76 P11, vol. 1, 234.1.5–234.1.6.

77 P4536, vol. 81, 155.1.6.

78 Bu-tön in his *Condensed General Presentation of the Tantra Sets* (Collected Works, Part 14 pha, (New Delhi, International Academy of Indian Culture, 1969), 895.2–895.7) explains this position and attributes it to Sö-nam-tse-mo who, without endorsing this view, presents it in his *General Presentation of the Tantra Sets* (sGang-tog, 'Bras-ljongs-sa-ngor-chos-tshogs, 1969), 27a. 4–30b.4.

79 Sö-nam-tse-mo is identified in the annotations to Bu-tön's *Condensed General Presentation of the Tantra Sets* (op. cit., 896.1–896.6); however, it is clear that Sö-nam-tse-mo is merely reporting this tradition without endorsing it in his *General Presentation of the Tantra Sets* (op. cit., 30b.4–31b.5).

80 Cone: rGyud gi 3a.2–4a.3. This corresponds with Bu-tön's explanation in his *Extensive General Presentation of the Tantra Sets* (Collected Works, Part 15 ba, (New Delhi, International Academy of Indian Culture, 1969), 35.7ff).

81 The explanation of the second begins on p. 162.

82 See pp. 161 and 201 for explanation.

83 The red and white minds of enlightenment, or vital essences of female and male.

84 Complete enjoyment, union, great bliss, non-inherent existence, compassion, uninterrupted continuity, and non-cessation.

85 P2328, vol. 55, 207.4.8–207.5.2.

86 Cone: rGyud ga 291b.3–291b.5.

87 In this context a seal is a hand sign, which is like a person's seal on a document in that it guarantees what it symbolises, here guaranteeing Tara's capacity to bestow Buddhahood.

88 P2328, vol. 55, 201.5.2.

89 P3333, vol. 71, 146.1.5.

90 P4530, vol. 81, 117.3.3–117.3.5.

91 Cone: rGyud nyu 65b.4.

92 The yoga of non-duality of the profound (emptiness) and the manifest (appearance as a deity).

93 Cone: rGyud nyu 65b.5.

94 P4530, vol. 81, 117.3.5–117.3.6.

95 Retention mantras are mantras for the sake of retaining words and meanings without forgetting them as well as for keeping one from falling to bad migrations.

96 Tsong-ka-pa identifies 'mantra' (see etymology of mantra on p. 106 here as primarily the bestowal of initiation which protects the mind from the suffering of bad migrations and so forth (P6187, vol. 160, 50.1.3).

97 Cone: rGyud ngi 233b.6–234a.2.

98 P2668, vol. 61, 295.1.4–295.1.5.

99 The general sources for the first two topics of the supplement are Jam-yang-shay-ba's *Great Exposition of Tenets* (Musoorie, Dalama, 1962) and Kön-chok-jig-may-wang-po's condensation of it in his *Precious Garland of Tenets* (Dharamsala, Shes-rig-par-khang, 1969). See Hopkins's forthcoming *Meditation on Emptiness* (New York, Nicolas Hays, Ltd.) for extensive explanation and the sources in detail. Below, the source for a Hinayana rendition of the Bodhisattva path is Tak-tsang's *An Explanation of 'Freedom from Extremes' in 'Revelation of All Tenets', An Ocean of Eloquence* (photographic reprint in the possession of Khetsun Sangpo, place and date of publication unknown), 28a.5.

100 This section particularly depends on the oral teachings of Kensur Lekden (1900–1971) as well as the two general sources mentioned in the previous note.

101 Jam-yang-shay-ba, *Great Exposition of the Middle Way* (Buxaduor, Gomang, 1967), 192b.2.

102 Op. cit., 14a.4–14b.3.

103 (Gangtok, Dodrup Chen Rinpoche, 1969 (?)), 137a.5–137b.2.

104 Ibid., 136a.1–136a.6.

105 *Presentation of the General Teaching and the Four Tantra Sets,* Collected Works, vol. IV (New Delhi, Gurudeva, 1973), 17b.5–18a.1.

106 See note 80.

107 *Presentation of the General Teaching and the Four Tantra Sets,* op. cit., 17a.2–17a.4.

108 The indented passages on this tradition are paraphrases of Sö-nam-tse-mo's *General Presentation of the Tantra Sets* (op. cit., 30b.4–31b.5) and Bu-tön's *Condensed General Presentation of the Tantra Sets* (op. cit., 89b.6ff).

109 *General Presentation of the Tantra Sets, Captivating the Wise,* Collected Works, vol. 11 (Darjeeling, Kargyud Sungrab Nyamso Khang, 1974), 16a.5.

110 *Presentation of the General Teaching and the Four Tantra Sets,* op. cit., 17b.1–17b.3.

111 *Explanation of the Rite of the Guhyasamaja Mandala* (New Delhi, Tanzin Kunga, 1972), 17.2–18.2.

112 *Clear Exposition of the Presentations of Tenets, A Beautiful Ornament for the Meru of the Subduer's Teaching* (Varanasi, The Pleasure of Elegant Sayings Printing Press, 1970), 529.18–530.8.

113 *Presentation of the General Teaching and the Four Tantra Sets*, op. cit., 17b.1–17b.3.
114 Ibid., 7b.2–7b.3.
115 Ibid., 8a.3.

Index